RACE AND RECKONING

ALSO BY ELLIS COSE

RACE AND RECKONING

FROM FOUNDING FATHERS
TO TODAY'S DISRUPTORS

ELLIS COSE

AMISTAD
An Imprint of HarperCollins*Publishers*

HarperCollins books may be purchased for educational, business, or sales promotional use. For information, please email the Special Markets Department at SPsales@harpercollins.com.

FIRST EDITION

Designed by Joy O'Meara @ Creative Joy Designs

Library of Congress Cataloging-in-Publication Data has been applied for.

ISBN 978-0-06-307244-2

22 23 24 25 26 LSC 10 9 8 7 6 5 4 3 2 1

For Elisa,
May her generation get it right

CONTENTS

INTRODUCTION

THE WAR OVER WHO WE ARE

It's a monumental challenge few Americans saw coming. This unde-clared war on our democracy, on the very idea of an egalitarian multi-cultural society, would have been unfathomable a few years back. But that was before a conquered president refused to concede defeat and instead used angry propaganda, preposterous lawsuits, and the full weight of the presidency to try to stay in power. That was before a mob of hooligans who brought death and destruction to the US Capitol was praised by the leaders of the defeated president's party. That was before some nineteen states passed thirty laws targeting fictional voter fraud, potentially denying countless fully qualified Americans the right to vote.

What accounts for this assault on the machinery of our democ-racy? Why, a full year after the election, did 52 percent of Republicans (according to a Reuters/Ipsos poll) insist that Donald Trump had "rightfully won" and 28 percent of all respondents attribute Joe Biden's victory to "illegal voting or election rigging"? Why have so many Americans become so unwilling to accept the legitimacy of our own political process?

Part of the answer lies in the chaos of the Donald Trump presidency—and in the values Trump promoted. He was not only dedicated to breaking norms but opposed to the rule of law itself. He surrounded himself with cronies and crooks, more than a dozen of whom had been indicted or faced criminal charges by the time he ran for reelection. And after losing, he unleashed attacks unlike any previously seen on the integrity of the vote and the democratic system.

That contempt for democratic customs coupled with an unprecedented assault on the machinery of democracy left many of Trump's followers suspicious of the election process and hostile to anyone deemed complicit in "stealing" the presidential election.

Still, Trump is only a man. His actions would never have had the impact they did—in fact, would not even have been possible—without the willing participation of other politicians, officials he appointed, and a large swath of the American electorate.

How we got to where we are today has a lot to do with our rich and conflicted history. There are things in the American experience that made many of us extremely susceptible to the appeal of a person such as Trump.

A lot of people would prefer to simply forget that history—especially in regard to race. Let's just pretend that those troubling things never happened, they say in effect; let's let bygones be bygones, embrace our common humanity, and get on with our collective lives.

It would be great if life were so simple. But obviously our past affects our present. No one, after all, would argue for trying to solve the problem of pollution by ignoring all the pollution that occurred in the past and focusing only on the pollution occurring right now. In order to solve pollution, we have to deal with all the garbage, all the pollutants that have been building up for generations. By the same token, it's impossible to rationally discuss ending inequality without acknowledging the impact of racial discrimination in the past, beginning with our legacy of enslavement and the racial hierarchy that stemmed from it.

Instead of acknowledging that simple truth, some political advocates, particularly on the right, equate being reminded of the sins of the past with attacking or promoting ill will toward Whites. So we have to listen to wacky arguments condemning such things as critical race theory, an arcane field of legal scholarship that is not even taught to young children, when what the aggrieved activists really want is to shut down discussion of America's racial past, period.

Rather than acknowledge that reality, certain critics prefer to ravage the entire field of scholarship on race, which they insist is nothing more than catering to Black and Brown racial grievance. It is better, they believe, to accept the narrative that the battle of the Alamo was all about liberty—while ignoring the fact that it was also a battle about keeping Blacks enslaved. By the same alchemy, the war against the Union becomes a noble effort to protect southern customs and defend states' rights, not a desperate effort to keep millions of people forever subjugated.

In December 2021, *The Washington Post* ran a poignant and disturbing profile of a White teacher in rural Kingsport, Tennessee, who had been fired for suggesting to his overwhelming White students that "White privilege" was a reality. In articulating such a notion, the teacher had violated a recently passed Tennessee law. At least eleven Republican-led states, noted the *Post,* had passed laws or approved policies effectively banning the teaching of concepts or ideas about race that were scorned by many conservatives; and more states were considering such laws.

Even a novel by the acclaimed author Toni Morrison came under attack by advocates of historical ignorance. The novel, *Beloved,* is based, in part, on the true story of a women who fled slavery and killed her own child rather than subject her anew to enslavement.

A political activist wanted the book removed from the curriculum because it gave nightmares to her adolescent son. The mother essentially argued that it was better to suppress the woeful story than to expose vulnerable students to *Beloved*. Never mind that such exposure might provide valuable insights into why human bondage is so unspeakably horrible, and into how it spawned a culture of victim-blaming, defiance, and denial among its perpetrators and defenders.

The problem with such a whitewashing of history is that it leaves no meaningful context for understanding the political behavior we witness today. To understand the current efforts to disenfranchise likely Democratic voters, you have to understand what happened at the end of Reconstruction.

The idea that certain votes should not count—or, to be more precise, that certain Americans were more entitled to the vote than others—is as old as the idea of America itself. For that reason, it was easy for White southerners to convince themselves, in the aftermath of the Civil War, that the Union had made a mistake. Despite the ratification of the Fifteenth Amendment, which granted Black freedmen the right to vote, White southerners passed an array of measures designed to deny that right. And in those less racially enlightened times, they were not shy about taking credit for doing so.

In his inaugural address in December 1890, South Carolina governor-elect Benjamin Tillman praised the White effort to block Blacks from voting, thereby ensuring "the triumph of Democracy and White supremacy over mongrelism and anarchy, of civilization over barbarism." Even "our colored fellow citizens," he insisted, were thrilled with the outcome, which was why they had "absolutely refused to be led to the polls by their bosses." As a result, he maintained, "there is less prejudice and more kindly feeling between the white man and the black man in South Carolina than has existed at any time since 1868." That racial harmony is enhanced by Black marginalization remains a popular argument among those pushing for regressive policies.

In an 1898 interview with the *Los Angeles Times*, William McCorkle, a former governor of West Virginia, explained that Black political empowerment had led to "political, financial, and moral" ruin, forcing Whites to agree "without regard to politics . . . that the negro rule should then and there cease."

In 1899, the *Atlanta Constitution* congratulated Mississippi for "solving" the Black voter problem. The "solution" involved requiring payment of a poll tax as well as proof that prospective voters could read and understand any section of the Constitution chosen by the examiner. The "Mississippi Plan" had worked so well, reported the newspaper, that South Carolina had followed it almost to the letter. Louisiana, North Carolina, and Alabama had "other elements to contend with" but expected to achieve the same objective through "a somewhat different method."

The *Constitution* concluded, "There can be no questioning the fact that the Mississippi plan of restricting the suffrage works well. . . . Under its workings the great mass of the ignorant and illiterate are kept from exercising the privilege of suffrage." The newspaper acknowledged that requiring prospective voters to interpret the Constitution "places into the hands of the registering officer a large amount of power for discrimination" but added that it "does not fly in the face of the suffrage amendments . . . for there is no discrimination on account of race, color or previous condition of servitude."

Today, the language of voter suppression is considerably more refined than that used by southerners in the wake of Reconstruction, but the approach and the arguments are much the same. Instead of keeping illiterate Black "mongrels" from voting, today's measures target undocumented immigrants, felons, and other disreputable sorts, who are presumed to be disproportionately people of color, from supposedly committing fraud on an epic scale. And just like the laws from the post-Reconstruction era, the suppression measures are crafted to evade constitutional prohibitions of discrimination.

After signing a highly controversial bill restricting voting in Texas in September 2021, Governor Greg Abbott declared, "No one who is eligible to vote will be denied the opportunity to vote." But the new law "does . . . make it harder for people to cheat," he insisted.

The *Texas Tribune* reported that the legislation "specifically targets voting initiatives used by diverse, Democratic Harris County, the state's most populous, by banning overnight early voting hours and drive-thru voting—both of which proved popular among voters of color last year."

Almost immediately after the law passed, the League of United Latin American Citizens announced a lawsuit to block its implementation. "LULAC strongly opposes this attack on our voting rights and freedoms because they have one and only one purpose—to dilute our voice at the ballot box and continue to stop electoral change in Texas," said Domingo Garcia, president of LULAC.

———

I did not realize when I started this book how much it would end up focusing on race. Along the way I concluded that it had to, that America's defining difference, our central division, has always revolved around race—around the way we justified the suffering and sacrifices of persons deemed unworthy of human kindness, around rebellion against laws and policies that would give such people a voice or even a chance at a decent life.

In an analysis of the January 6, 2021, Capitol insurrection, University of Chicago researchers concluded that the violence had been driven largely by fear that "the rights of minorities and immigrants were crowding out the rights of white people." They also realized that the insurrection movement had been larger and more volatile than had previously been assumed. That, perhaps, should not have been surprising. Violence has regularly followed in the wake of perceived encroachment on White territory by threatening minorities. For many, the Barack Obama presidency was such an encroachment, as was the rejection, largely by voters in so-called blue states, of a president who had made White grievance the cornerstone of his message. Trump's campaign loudly endorsed the notion that the path to greatness was through recreating the past. It embraced, as heroes, the leaders of the Confederacy, whose army had fought to destroy not only Black ambition but to forcefully overthrow a duly elected president who deemed democracy and slavery incompatible with each other.

Since then, the advocacy of violence in certain political circles has grown. In a widely reported incident during a conservative political rally at Boise State University in Idaho in October 2021, a man stepped up to the microphone with some sharp observations and a question.

"At this point, we're living under corporate and medical fascism. This is tyranny," he declared. "When do we get to use the guns? . . . I mean, literally, where's the line? How many elections are they going to steal before we kill these people?" The sentiment was hauntingly similar to that of John Wilkes Booth, Abraham Lincoln's assassin. He complained that Lincoln's policies were dragging America "deeper and deeper into cruelty and oppression" and conflicted with the Founders' injunction "to hate tyranny, to love liberty and justice" and "to strike at wrong and oppression."

In recalling the Boise State incident, the *New York Times* observed, "threats of violence are becoming commonplace among a significant segment of the Republican Party." Although it was not exactly a threat, the circulating by Republican Congressman Paul Gosar of a video in which his avatar seemingly killed Congresswoman Alexandria Ocasio-

Cortez was seen by many as an example of just how violent and un-hinged much political dialogue has become.

We have been this way before, and one result was the Civil War.

———

Despite divisions that stretch back to before the time of Lincoln, Amer-icans of all races share a cultural identity and a belief in liberty. That is something we should celebrate. But we also have a history of separate-ness, of marginalizing those who are not White and shrinking from the notion of interracial equality.

We are now engaged in a war not just over that history but over which vision of America will prevail: the vision that rejects the idea that all Americans are equal or the vision that accepts all Americans as equally entitled to the privileges of citizenship.

As the nation wrestles with what has come to be called a "reckon-ing," it is essential that we make connections between the present and the past, that we understand what brought us to this present moment, that we realize that some of what troubles us today had its origins in another era. We are still arguing with the ghost of Thomas Jefferson, still debating the proper structure of a democracy. We are still discover-ing who we are and what we may yet be.

I do not pretend to have the answers; but I do see evidence of an emerging consciousness, of a growing array of people, perhaps a criti-cal mass, collectively asking what it will take to make us one nation. I find that both exciting and encouraging and take it as evidence that we increasingly may be ready to accept the proposition that progress does not mean denying or whitewashing our history but accepting and understanding it as we contemplate how to move forward.

1

CHOOSING SLAVERY

In August 2019, America commemorated the four hundredth anniversary of its first tentative step toward race-based slavery. It began with the arrival of a small group of Africans who reached Virginia's Jamestown colony on an English privateer—or government-commissioned pirate ship.

After landing in Jamestown, the *White Lion* bartered its cargo of "20 and odd Negroes" from Angola for "victuals," according to a letter from John Rolfe, an English settler and tobacco entrepreneur who had married Pocahontas, who subsequently became famous because of her importance to, and elevation within, White colonial society. Four days later, the *Treasurer* put in, also carrying captured Africans: the remainder of the human cargo seized from the *São João Bautista*, a slave ship bound for Mexico.

What became of those twice-taken Africans is not completely clear. Were they enslaved and condemned to a life of misery? Or were they given employment, with the possible prospect of becoming prosperous and free? Debate over that question has raged for more than a century.

What that debate makes clear is that slavery was not inevitable. It is something America chose over the course of decades.

The indentured servitude system came into existence shortly before the *White Lion* and the *Treasurer* showed up. Don Jordan and Michael Walsh, the authors of *White Cargo: The Forgotten History of Britain's White Slaves in America,* trace its beginnings to 1618, when street urchins from the slums of London were sent to Virginia to work in the fields.

The ranks of indentured servants quickly grew to include adult criminals and vagrants. "They ranged from beggars to prostitutes, Quakers to Cavaliers," write Jordan and Walsh. Migrants also came from Ireland: "Under Oliver Cromwell's ethnic-cleansing policy in Ireland, unknown numbers of Catholic men, women and children were forcibly transported to the colonies." Others were kidnapped from the streets of England and forced onto ships. The majority, however, came willingly, hoping that free passage and the possible gift of land in the colonies would allow them to start anew. "Between 1620 and 1775, these volunteer servants, some 300,000, accounted for two out of three migrants from the British Isles," claim Jordan and Walsh.

A few of the servants did very well. The most celebrated, a Dutchman indentured to a wealthy Dutch family, became the progenitor of the famous Vanderbilt family. Jan Aertsen van der Bilt, whose passage was paid by the Dutch West India Company, arrived in America around 1650. After serving his period of bondage, he acquired a small farm on Long Island. His descendant Cornelius Vanderbilt, born in 1794, became the prototypical American tycoon, amassing a fortune worth billions in today's dollars.

No African newcomers had the luck of the Vanderbilts. But their lot was not altogether hopeless. Indeed, some "became artisans; a few became landowners and the masters of other men," noted the historians Oscar and Mary F. Handlin.

The most famous was Antonio, an Angolan who appears to have arrived in Virginia in the early 1600s and became known as Anthony Johnson.

Johnson, who worked as an indentured servant, was eventually freed and acquired 250 acres of farmland and five indentured servants, including John Casor. In late 1653, Casor complained to Samuel Goldsmith, a White visitor to Johnson's property, that he was being illegally held beyond the period of his indenture. Goldsmith shared the conversation with Johnson's neighbors, George and Robert Parker. The Parker brothers encouraged Casor to sue for his freedom. Casor followed their advice and the Parkers warned Johnson that Casor might be awarded his cows if he prevailed. Unnerved by that possibility, Johnson acceded to the court's order to release Casor, who went to work for Robert Parker.

Johnson almost immediately had a change of heart. He sued Parker in county court, claiming that his neighbor "detains one John Casor, a Negro [and] the plaintiff's Servant under pretense" that Casor "is a free man."

The judge agreed and, in March 1655, he ordered that Casor be returned to Johnson, his "right master," and extended Casor's length of service to life. He also ordered Parker to pay court costs.

"This was the first civil case in which a Virginia court made a black indentured servant a slave," according to history professor Edgar Toppin. In so doing, the court turned a former Black indentured servant into one of the first slave owners in Virginia, notes historian Steve Byas.

The existence of free Black men such as Johnson is remarkable in light of how Africans and their descendants eventually came to be treated. For a period, before the march toward race-based slavery became irrepressible, colonial leaders did not object to Blacks suing Whites or testifying against them in court, or even to Whites working for Blacks. That changed over the years as various paths to freedom for Blacks were eliminated.

In 1662, Virginia ruled out having a White father as grounds for emancipation. In 1667, freedom through baptism was disposed of. In 1705, Virginia's General Assembly passed a series of measures denying Blacks dignity and humanity. Whites were given permission to kill the enslaved with impunity. As the statute put it: "If any slave resists his master . . . and shall happen to be killed in such correction . . . the master shall be free of all punishment . . . as if such accident never happened." The notion that any amount of violence was justified in taming uncooperative Blacks is one of many ideas, marinated in slavery, that managed to survive beyond slavery itself.

Intermarriage was prohibited. White women who bore children fathered by Black, Native American, or mulatto men were subject to fines and their children condemned to servitude. And "all negro, mulatto, and Indian slaves" were deemed property that could be inherited by widows and heirs just like real estate.

That Africans were forced into slavery while indentured Whites retained their freedom was partly because subjugating Africans was so much easier than enslaving Whites. Turning White settlers into slaves would have been a monumental task given their ties to countrymen who were free, their ability to vanish into the general population, and Great Britain's opposition to slavery. Indeed, even keeping the flow of European indentured servants coming meant treating them well enough that they didn't warn others away. Africans had no such leverage.

But before the colonies could fully embrace race-based slavery, they had to create a form of racism noxious enough to obliterate moral qualms about treating human beings as beasts. So as the country evolved, theories supporting racism also evolved—enough to accommodate the contradiction of creating a nation based on the concept of human equality even as it denied the humanity of huge groups of people. Americans essentially came to argue, as the journalist Angela

Saini put it, that Blacks were enslaved because the status of slave "was their biological place in the universe." And no public figure was more adept at making that argument than Thomas Jefferson.

In *Notes on the State of Virginia*, Jefferson's only published book, he ruminated about how "fine mixtures of red and white" are clearly preferable to "that eternal monotony" of Blackness, and on how "flowing hair" with its "elegant symmetry of form" led even Blacks to prefer White women to their own. He commented on Blacks' "very strong and disagreeable odour" and the supposed fact that they required less sleep—even after hard labor—than did Whites. He observed that Blacks' grief was transient, that Black love "kindles the senses only, not the imagination," and that Blacks seemed incapable of uttering "a thought above the level of plain narration."

Jefferson, in short, made the case that such creatures, who had more in common with orangutans than humans, had been done a favor by allowing them to serve as slaves.

As enslavement flourished, the indentured servitude system withered. Whereas roughly half of Europeans landing in British North America during the 1700s had financed their voyage through labor contracts, the indentured servitude model essentially vanished in the early nineteenth century. That was not just because of competition from enslaved labor but because "superior methods of financing migration developed," as the economist Farley Grubb put it. One such method was simply borrowing money from people who had already made it to America.

The decision to embrace enslavement over compensated servitude foreclosed the possibility of a Black Vanderbilt arising. More important, it put America on a road of perpetual friction and inequality that sits at the center of a multitude of vexing problems that, on the surface, have nothing to do with race.

———

Before African enslavement became common, before the rules became rigid, Native American bondage was given a try. Forced Native American labor was a profitable practice for the Spaniards—although they rarely described the practice as slavery. They were more comfortable calling their system *encomienda* (meaning entrustment or entrust: essentially a form of compelled labor or dominion over conquered communities that was permitted by the Spanish Crown).

Among the English, Native American enslavement was easily rationalized. They reasoned that offering captives taken in a "just war" the option of enslavement was morally sound, since slavery was better than death. Also, the Native American practice of "raiding for captives" had made enslavement familiar to certain tribes, argued Alan Gallay, the author of *The Indian Slave Trade: The Rise of the English Empire in the American South, 1670–1717*.

King Philip's War in New England in 1675 and 1676 resulted in hundreds of Native Americans being sold abroad as slaves. Bacon's Rebellion, a settler revolt in Virginia in 1676, ended with yet more Native Americans enslaved. But it was in South Carolina that the slave trade flourished. By the early eighteenth century, noted the legal scholar Gregory Ablavsky, the state's traffic in enslaved Native Americans rivaled its trade in enslaved Africans.

Native Americans were also slave owners and slave trackers, and many intermarried with Blacks—depending on the tribe, location, and circumstance.

As African enslavement became a defining fixture of American life, the appetite for Native American slaves diminished—largely because it came with such downsides, including the ever-present possibility of war against the colonists. Settlers also believed that Native Americans were more likely to run away, more likely to die from their labors, and less effective workers than Africans.

By the late 1700s, Native American slavery had largely run its course. In 1772, Founding Father George Mason represented a group of twelve plaintiffs descended from Native American women who contended that their mothers' ethnicity made their enslavement illegal. Mason also contended that the enslavement of Native Americans violated God's law, making the statute permitting such enslavement "void."

The court declined to rule on the will of God but agreed that Native American enslavement was illegal since the law authorizing it had been repealed. The plaintiffs were freed and granted court costs and nominal damages. That decision foreshadowed the demise of Native American enslavement—even as colonial leaders continued to defend the enslavement of Blacks.

Allowing Native Americans to petition for freedom served an important psychological purpose for American colonists, argued Gregory Ablavsky. The near impossibility of winning freedom through a court—which entailed producing myriad documents and hiring a sympathetic White attorney—meant that extremely few enslaved Native Americans could avail themselves of the remedy. But the very possibility, slim though it was, "reassured anxious Virginians that, despite failing to eliminate African slavery, their society was committed to emancipatory principles."

Nevertheless, applying those principles differently to different groups meant engaging in some formidable mental gymnastics, especially since Whites were not required to prove anything to avoid enslavement. It meant, as a minimum, accepting a belief in racial differences—and a racial hierarchy—even while arguing for the equality of man.

As noted previously, Jefferson firmly believed that Blacks were incapable of self-government or intellectual achievement, whereas he believed Native Americans had excellent potential. With none of the advantages given to Blacks, Native Americans "will often carve figures on their pipes not destitute of design and merit. They will crayon out an animal, a plant, or a country, so as to prove the existence of a germ in their minds which only wants cultivation," he wrote.

Jefferson owned hundreds of Black slaves. He was duty bound to justify their subjugation. He did so by insisting that they were deficient human beings who lacked the potential to be anything more than slaves. He was not similarly compelled to justify the enslavement of Native Americans. His five-thousand-acre plantation, after all, was not maintained by an enslaved Native American labor force.

But despite Jefferson's admiration of Native Americans, he considered them culturally incompatible and was not opposed to their removal—especially if they refused assimilation and civilization. In an 1803 letter to Indiana Territory governor William Henry Harrison, Jefferson observed that valuable land was in Native American hands and floated the idea of forcing tribes into debt in order for the US government to acquire it. He also opined that ultimately, Native Americans were left with two options: they could either "incorporate with us as citizens" or be forced to relocate "beyond the Mississippi."

The issue of what to do with the Native Americans became increasingly urgent in the early 1800s as White settlers covetously eyed Native American–occupied land in various parts of the South. In an 1809 meeting in Washington, DC, President Jefferson suggested to a Cherokee delegation that those Native Americans who preferred to pursue life as hunters instead of farmers might be better off out west in "some of the vacant lands of the United States, where game is abundant." Eight years later, Jefferson was no longer in office, but his proposal was formalized in an 1817 treaty in which the Sioux swapped land in the East for land along the Arkansas River—an agreement seen by some scholars as the beginning of the era of "Indian removal."

By that point, White settlers had decided that their desire for the land took precedence over any Native American claims, and the so-called Five Civilized Tribes—Cherokee, Choctaw, Chickasaw, Creek or Muskogee, and Seminole—were in the way. The "Civilized Tribes" were so called because, as Whites saw it, they had adopted certain White customs and were willing to coexist with Whites. Although they were not as civilized as Anglo-Saxons, explained the *St. Louis Post Dispatch*, they had "abandoned the wild, roving life of the ordinary Indian and have shown a disposition to settle down and live in houses."

By 1829, Indian removal had become de facto US policy. That February, the Senate Committee on Indian Affairs formally adopted the government's removal proposal.

Andrew Jackson, who had become president that year, suggested to Congress in December that the tribes, in order to avoid annihilation, should abandon their claims on their land in the South. He promised that "emigration would be voluntary," since it would be "cruel and unjust to compel the aborigines to abandon the graves of their fathers and seek a home in a distant land."

In May 1930, as the so-called Indian Removal Act ("A Bill to provide for the removal of the Indian tribes within any of the States and Territories, and for their permanent settlement West of the river Mississippi") approached a vote, Congressman Wilson Lumpkin of Georgia urged his colleagues to pass it. "Reject it, and you leave them to perish," he argued.

Many progressives and religious groups fought the effort. Activists "organized the first national women's petition campaign and flooded Congress with antiremoval petitions," according to the historian Mary Hershberger. Nonetheless, the Indian Removal Act passed Congress on May 26, 1830, and President Jackson signed it into law two days later. Soon thereafter, a substantial portion of America's Native American population was moved west. As the historian Angie Debo put it, "By a combination of bribery, trickery, and intimidation the Federal agents induced all five tribes during the 1830s to cede the remainder of their Eastern lands to the United States and to agree to migrate beyond the Mississippi." The process took nearly a decade, with the Choctaw going first and the Cherokee last.

The removal process had begun even before the Removal Act cleared Congress. In 1828, Georgia had passed a series of laws that had stripped the Native Americans of various rights and lands, declaring that all lands "within the conventional limits of Georgia, belong to her absolutely" and pronouncing the Native Americans "tenants at her will." The legislature also asked President Jackson to take whatever steps would be required for the "extinguishment" of Cherokee titles "to all or any part of the lands now in their possession, within the limits of Georgia."

The Cherokees had rejected Georgia's claim, arguing that colonists had no right to the land previously "inhabited exclusively by Indians of various tribes" and that the colonies had been installed "without the consent or knowledge" of the original inhabitants.

The matter ended up before the US Supreme Court, which suggested in *Cherokee Nation v. Georgia* (1831) that the Cherokee had a right to their land but also concluded that the Court did not have jurisdiction. The Cherokee Nation had filed for relief as a foreign state, but the Supreme Court was not sure that it was entitled to that status. To the court, the Cherokee seemed to constitute a "domestic dependent nation," which meant that the justices could not decide the case as filed. Although the Cherokee saw the Court's opinion as a victory, the US government ignored it and proceeded to push the Native Americans out.

The discovery of gold on Cherokee land in Georgia had made the Cherokee position especially perilous. "The first gold mines in north Georgia opened in the summer of 1829, and by autumn the region was flooded with gold-hungry prospectors," noted the historian David Williams. Yelverton King, a lawyer appointed by the governor of Georgia to investigate the local situation, described prospectors behaving in a "riotous and disorderly manner." Debo wrote of their "tearing down the Indians' fences and destroying their crops."

As fortune hunters poured in, Native Americans were pushed aside. Most of the Cherokee Nation "was raffled off in a land lottery from which the Indians themselves were barred," noted Williams. The Cherokee sought justice in the Supreme Court, which ruled that Georgia had exceeded its authority. But the government rolled ahead with its plans.

In 1835, with no relief in sight and officials at all levels of government pushing them to go, some members of the Cherokee Nation signed the so-called Treaty of New Echota. The treaty pledged "perpetual peace and friendship" between the United States and the Cherokee Nation and offered a financial settlement to the Cherokee, who at that point were desperate.

The Treaty of New Echota was contested by tribe members who claimed that the negotiators did not represent them. The disaffected group went to Washington and asked the Senate to kill the treaty. Instead, the Senate ratified it.

Still, some Cherokee refused to leave. "So, in 1838," wrote Professor Robert Watson in the *South Florida Sun-Sentinel*, "General Winfield Scott, hero of the War of 1812, was sent to Georgia with 7,000 troops, who proceeded to round up the Cherokee at bayonet point. [More than] 16,000 Cherokees were sent west. Cholera, dysentery, typhus and starvation claimed thousands of lives during the journey."

The so-called Trail of Tears has become the stuff of legend. The historian Theda Perdue argued that the phrase misrepresents reality by collapsing a tragic historical episode "into one sentimental narrative featuring the Cherokees . . . while . . . denying the suffering of many other native peoples" and absolving southerners of responsibility "for the plight of Indians who remained."

Like enslavement of Africans, the removal of Native Americans, which effectively made the US a White country, was a deliberate choice—and one made against the loud objections of those who thought it shortsighted and morally unacceptable. It was also, as Perdue suggested, a decision that was poorly carried out, imposing unspeakable suffering on those who left as well as those who stayed.

It was only a matter of time before the western promised land was sacrificed to avarice. In the early 1900s, some seventy thousand Native Americans owned roughly half of what would become the state of Oklahoma. As more and more Whites moved in, the government broke its carefully negotiated treaties and pushed the Native Americans aside. "Within a generation these Indians, who had owned and governed a region greater in area and potential wealth than many an American state, were almost stripped of their holdings. . . . Such treatment of an independent people by a great imperial power would have aroused international condemnation; but these Indian republics were . . . 'domestic dependent nations,'" observed Debo.

In 1907, Oklahoma became a state. Legislation that passed Congress in April 1906 dissolved tribal courts and other such institutions while paving the way for statehood, which included converting "each individual tribesman . . . from a ward of the government into a citizen," in the words of the *Detroit Free Press*.

In its coverage of the law's passage, the *Detroit Free Press* included a commentary by Charles Eastman—an activist, physician, and author of books on Native American heritage whom the newspaper incorrectly identified as a "a full-blooded Sioux." (Eastman, a graduate of Boston Medical School, also claimed English and French ancestry.)

Eastman confessed that he did not believe "in trying to delay the inevitable absorption of my race into the dominant white race of this country. The sooner that absorption is accomplished, the sooner the 'Indian question' comes to an end.

"Now the problem for my race is how best to adapt itself to the conditions belonging to the white man's civilization . . . and hence, to emancipate itself from its present degraded position."

Eastman revealed that he had been engaged by the government "on a rather novel undertaking": he had been charged with renaming Native Americans, giving them names more congenial to the White man's tongue. He estimated that it would take him "about two years more to finish this strange mission," which he apparently found quite satisfying: "It is only one step in making my people realize the importance of hastening their absorption by the white race, and, as far as it goes, it is of value in making them appreciate the value of practical things in bearing the white man's burden."

Eastman, a sophisticated man, no doubt realized that part of the White man's burden was making sure that White men stayed on top, and presumably he had concluded that "absorption" was not just "inevitable" but significantly more desirable than annihilation.

2

A VANISHING MIDDLE GROUND

The Civil War is not something Americans got into by mistake, because of a simple misunderstanding, or for lack of interest in compromise. And although it was a struggle over states' rights, that was true only in a very narrow sense. At its root, it was always a fight—and what proved to be an irreconcilable conflict—over one thing. Abraham Lincoln identified that thing with precision in a speech he gave in Illinois after receiving the Republican nomination for the Senate in 1858.

"I believe this government cannot endure, permanently half slave and half free," he said. God knows, the country had been trying to do so since its founding. But in the 1800s, a series of decisions and opportunities drove the country to the breaking point. America was forced to choose: either slavery was immoral, or it was not; either it should be allowed in the western territories, or it should not; either enslaved persons were human beings and therefore entitled to rights, or they were a species of subhumans whose only useful function was to service their superiors.

The problem was that once having gone down a fundamentally immoral path, the nation had a hard time squaring that decision with its professed beliefs. So it made endless compromises with itself—in order to ease its conscience, maintain its uncompensated workforce, and avoid an obvious truth: that it was addicted to something evil.

The Compromise of 1820 was one in a series of such compromises. It allowed the entrance of Maine into the Union as a free state and Missouri as a slave state, maintaining the balance in the Senate between free and slave. The compromise also prohibited the formation of new slave states north of the southern Missouri line.

The deal, orchestrated by Speaker of the House Henry Clay, required more than the usual arm-twisting because many legislators were aghast at the idea of Congress sanctioning the expansion of slavery. But ultimately they fell in line.

Thirty years later, Clay, by then a senator, again offered a compromise over slavery. The so-called Compromise of 1850 was negotiated in the wake of the California Gold Rush and dealt with the lands, including California, that had been acquired in the Mexican-American War.

Clay, a former secretary of state then in his early seventies, fully appreciated the difficulty of the selling job before him. "I have witnessed many periods of great anxiety, of peril, and of danger even to the country; but I have never before arisen to address any assembly so oppressed, so appalled, so anxious," he told his Senate colleagues in February 1850.

"Eight years ago, I took my leave finally, and—as I supposed—forever of this body," he said. But the "legislature of the state to which I belong, unsolicited by me, chose to designate me to represent them in this Senate; and I have come here in obedience to a sense of stern duty, with no personal objects—no private views now or hereafter to gratify."

The press treated Clay's appearance as if he were a returning rock star. "Mr. Clay finished today his great speech. It lasted about two hours and a half, and it came fully up to his best efforts of former times," commented the *Baltimore Sun*. Clay's plan consisted of eight resolutions that took on the basically unanswerable question of how the United States could remain a nation where freedom and slavery coexisted.

For the next several months, Congress struggled to follow Clay's template, but a harsh reality loomed over the process. As the abolitionist *National Era* observed that March, "The equilibrium is already destroyed. Delaware, nominally a slave State, to all intents and purposes cooperates with the free. . . . And, in a few years a large number of new free States will be knocking for admission, while every year the slaveholding interest is decreasing."

The *Baltimore Sun* was skeptical of the evolving compromise, observing in mid-July, "The bill has assumed the shape in which it cannot very well be improved by amendments; for what these amendments gain with the opponents of the bill they lose with its supporters." In early September the legislation, consisting of five separate bills, passed Congress, which the *Sun* interpreted as a sign that "the glorious prospect of peace . . . is now dawning upon the country."

Under the compromise, California would be admitted as a free state. The slave trade (but not slavery itself) would be prohibited in the District of Columbia. Texas's western and northern borders were set, enabling the federal government to take territory previously claimed by Texas.

The Fugitive Slave Act, the most contested part of the compromise package, passed last. President Millard Fillmore signed the legislation into law on September 18, 1850. Canada's *Globe and Mail* dryly observed, "A bill has been passed converting the Free States into Slave-catchers of the runaway chattels of the South. . . . What would be thought in Canada, if an Imperial and Local Act were passed converting all the inhabitants of our free Canada into slave-hunters." The

Liberator complained, "the bill converts all the officers of the General Government . . . into official slave-catchers."

Fighting the law became a cause célèbre. Some escapees became celebrities.

According to several contemporary publications, the first fugitive arrested was James Hamlet (also known as James Hamilton Williams), who, in 1848, had fled from Baltimore to New York City, where he became a shopkeeper. An agent working for Mary Brown, his former owner, located Hamlet in New York in 1850 and demanded his arrest. At the subsequent hearing, Brown's son-in-law testified that Brown was "entitled to Hamlet's services, as a slave, for life. She never parted with him voluntarily."

"When Hamlet was arrested, he gave a signal to a number of colored persons in the neighborhood, and but for the presence of a number of officers, he would have been taken from the Deputy Marshall by force," reported the *Republican Banner,* which observed that several hundred Blacks gathered around the jail to express outrage. The crowd was "put on a wrong scent. But for this a riot would no doubt have ensued," speculated the *Banner.*

Once Hamlet was returned to Baltimore, Brown announced that she was willing to sell him to his friends in New York. "The money was instantly raised by subscription, and the ransomed Hamlet was brought back in triumph," reported *The Observer* of London.

Shortly thereafter a rally was held in Hamlet's honor during which a biracial array of speakers lambasted the Fugitive Slave Act.

William Powell, a prominent abolitionist who chaired the event, declared that the Fugitive Slave Act, "this covenant with death, this agreement with hell, must be trampled underfoot and violated for all hazards." The Rev. Charles Gardner, a Black abolitionist from Philadelphia, advised Blacks to kill "any man who attempted to arrest them." A Black Methodist minister, identified only as Mr. Raymond, also addressed the crowd. "Hamlet . . . whose freedom had been purchased by paying $800 to the slave-catcher, stood at the right of Raymond, and tears ran down his cheeks, while the speaker addressed the horrors of slavery," reported the *New York Evangelist*.

Three years after the law's passage, controversy over the captured formerly enslaved was still going strong. In Cincinnati, in 1853, "a mulatto who calls himself George McCreary," who had escaped bondage four years earlier, went to court to fight his forcible return to Kentucky, reported the *Louisville Courier Journal*. The proceedings attracted a large interracial crowd. The judge decided that he had no alternative but to return George to his former master, who offered to sell him at a discounted price to those wishing to purchase his freedom. It's unclear whether anyone accepted his offer.

Meanwhile, the battle over slavery focused on the Kansas-Nebraska Act of 1854. The legislation, authored by Illinois senator Stephen Douglas, embraced the concept of "popular sovereignty." In other words, residents of the territories seeking statehood would themselves decide whether their state was to be slave or free. Douglas hoped that the measure would stabilize the situation out west in order to facilitate the construction of the transcontinental railroad. But instead of ending the debate over slavery, it took it to a new, more violent level as settlers fought over whether the territory would be slave or free. One of the more dramatic episodes occurred in Lawrence, Kansas, on May 21, 1856.

Founded in 1854, with the support of wealthy abolitionist Amos Lawrence, the city quickly became a free-state haven. By 1856, Lawrence's roughly fifteen hundred residents had become renowned defenders of the anti-slavery cause. The Free State Hotel, the town's main gathering spot, also known as the Eldridge House, was widely rumored to be an armory full of weapons dedicated to the defense of abolitionists.

On that Wednesday morning in May, deputy US marshal William Perry Fain and a small posse visited the hotel to arrest some of Lawrence's most prominent figures for treason in their defiance of territorial authorities. The proprietor, Shalor Eldridge, informed Fain that only two of the suspects were on the premises. The two, George Washington Deitzler and George W. Smith, surrendered peacefully. Fain and his men ate lunch at the hotel, and Eldridge delivered the two prisoners in his personal hack to the posse encampment outside of town.

That afternoon, as the temperature soared past 90 degrees, Douglas County sheriff Samuel Jones rode into Lawrence. As described by *New York Times* special correspondent William "Randolph" Hutchinson, Jones and his posse "came marching into town with all manner of flags waving in the breeze. On one was borne in large letters the inscription, 'The Equality of the White Race,' upon one side, and on the other 'Kansas the out-post.' "

Jones had been publicly embarrassed in Lawrence the previous month. He had arrested Samuel Wood, part owner of the *Kansas Tribune*, for helping a free-stater escape justice. But a mob forced Wood's release. Jones later returned with a posse but was unable to track down Wood. That night, while resting, the sheriff was wounded by an unknown assailant.

"We were surprised to see him in riding condition so soon; but, on seeing him nearer, he appeared quite emaciated and pale," reported the *Times*. At the hotel, Jones summoned Samuel Clarke Pomeroy, a town founder and chairman of the Lawrence Committee of Public Safety, to whom he delivered a short speech.

"I have come here today to make a demand of this town. I have often tried to make arrests, and the last time I was here came near losing my life. I, therefore, as the US Marshal for Kansas Territory, and as Sheriff of Douglas Country, demand of you all your arms. Bring out your rifles and stack them in the street, and carry your cannon to the field yonder where you see our men. I will give you just five minutes for an answer," declared Jones.

Jones returned roughly a half hour later. Pomeroy had produced one howitzer and three breach-loading cannons. The hotel possessed no other armaments except those in private hands, Pomeroy insisted.

In response, the posse moved down the hill and placed four cannons "where they could rake the entire business part of the town," reported the *Times*.

Despite his confident assertion of authority, Jones was not, in any literal sense, a US Marshal, although the actual US Marshal had allowed Jones to assume command of his men. Professor Pearl Ponce, editor of *Kansas's War: The Civil War in Documents*, contends that Jones "falsely claiming federal duty" led "what had become a mob into town." That mob "smashed the newspaper presses, burned the Free State Hotel and other buildings, and terrified Lawrence residents. Because of confusion as to whether Jones was executing a federal order, these actions seemed to have the patina of federal approval," argues Ponce.

It was certainly an odd situation, which made it difficult for residents to know whether Jones was conducting a sanctioned federal operation or carrying out a personal vendetta. As the *Times* correspondent cynically observed, "Sheriff Jones summoned them all as his posse—to do I know not what—and he became supreme commander of the red host."

The *Times* correspondent claimed "the Hotel was bombarded for an hour and afterwards burnt. . . . No lives were lost today, but I fear the worst."

Over the next few days, the national press anguished over what it portrayed as the annihilation of Lawrence. "The Town of Lawrence Bombarded and Reduced to Ashes," declared the *New York Herald Tribune*. The newspaper also claimed that several persons were "slaughtered." "A Battle at Lawrence—Loss of Life on Both Sides," claimed the *Baltimore Sun*.

That report was mistaken. The one documented fatality was of a member of the posse who reportedly died after being struck by a falling brick from the collapsing hotel. Nonetheless, many came to view the attack on Lawrence as the first real battle of the Civil War. It left a legacy of immense bitterness and ignited widespread violence, paving the way for the so-called Lawrence massacre of 1863 (during which a

Confederate guerrilla group slaughtered some 150 male residents). It also apparently moved abolitionist John Brown to revenge.

Days after the assault on Lawrence, armed men attacked proslavery settlers at Pottawatomie Creek. A congressional committee concluded that the abolitionist John Brown had been responsible for the ambush and murder of five proslavery advocates that night. Martin Franklin Conway, a judge and an acquaintance of Brown who served as Kansas's first member of Congress, said Brown told him "that he was not at the killing, but he approved it." No one was ever tried for the crime.

The Kansas-Nebraska dispute splintered the Whig Party and spawned the Republican Party, which called for the repeal of the Fugitive Slave Act and dedicated itself to stopping the spread of slavery.

In a July 1854 editorial, the Democratic *Detroit Free Press* responded with indignation, calling the new Republican Party a "bastard issue of illicit intercourse" that "will die young and have an early burial."

Much of the media took to calling members of the new party "Black Republicans." The term, meant as an insult, was a reminder that, on the question of slavery, the party sided with Blacks over Whites. The *American Organ*, a "Know Nothing" publication, explained, "Those French desperadoes who design the destruction of life and property are called Red Republicans. Why should not be the reckless advocates of abolition and disunion be called the Black Republicans? . . . The sole subject of agitation and declamation, with this party, is the condition of the negroes."

The *Cincinnati Daily Inquirer* warned readers that a vote for the "Black Republican ticket" was tantamount to saying that Blacks should be allowed to vote, hold office, sit on juries, and enjoy "all the rights and privileges of citizens."

John C. Frémont, an explorer, Mexican-American War hero, and former California senator, was the 1856 Republican presidential candidate. His slogan was "Free Soil, Free Labor, Free Speech, Free Men, and Frémont," or variations, sometimes including the phrase, "Free Speech." He ran against Millard Fillmore, a former president and former Whig representing the American (or "Know Nothing") Party, and Democrat James Buchanan, a former secretary of state.

Although Frémont was relentlessly attacked as a radical whose election would destroy the Union, he won a majority of the free-state votes, coming in second behind Buchanan, who won the Electoral College majority.

Despite Frémont's loss, the issue of slavery continued to roil the nation and enthrall the press—which entertained readers with tales of escaped Blacks and their attempted recapture. In 1856, the case of "Peggy" attracted wide attention. After fleeing to Ohio, Peggy had slit her daughter's throat rather than see the child returned to slavery in Kentucky. Among the many questions raised by the case was a rather novel one: as one correspondent put it, "If the mother is detained as a murderess and the adults as accessories, can the children be sent back?" They were, and a second child of Peggy, an infant, drowned during the journey.

During the trial, the *New York Daily Times,* attempted to humanize Peggy with personal details. It explained that she originally had been brought from Kentucky to Ohio when she was only seven years old in order to care for her master's child. The *Times* also noted that she was pregnant, which apparently had evoked sympathy among certain members of the public: "Some ladies, living near the jail, prepared a few delicacies for the pregnant woman, Peggy, but were not allowed by the jailor to give them to her. The diet is limited to bean soup and baker's bread." The paper also revealed that the escape from Kentucky may have been abetted by Whites: "Two amiable English ladies . . . were suspected of having told these colored people of the chances of escape, and were obliged to leave Kentucky very hastily . . . to escape lynching!" The *Times* dwelled on Peggy's appearance and that of her dead child, who was "almost white" and "a little girl of rare beauty." Peggy herself was "about five feet three inches in height, and rather stoutly than delicately made. She is a mulatto, showing from one-fourth to one-third white blood. . . . Her eyebrows are delicate lines, finely arched; and her eyes, though not remarkably large, are bright and intelligent. . . . She is twenty-two or three years of age." The paper described scars on Peggy's forehead: "We asked how those scars came there. She said, 'White man struck me.'"

"Peggy," whose full name was Margaret Garner, was the inspiration for *Beloved,* a novel by Nobel Prize winner Toni Morrison. Glenn Youngkin, the winning candidate in the 2021 Virginia governor's race, ran ads championing a mother who insisted that Morrison's novel had given her son nightmares and wanted such works banned from certain public-school curricula.

———

In March 1857, the Supreme Court decided the Dred Scott case.

The central question was whether Scott's "owners" had inadvertently freed him by taking him from a slave state (Missouri) into a free state and free territories. The 7–2 decision, authored by Chief Justice Roger Taney, concluded that they had not. Because of his race, neither Scott nor his "fellow African Americans were or could be citizens," concluded Taney. And since Scott was not a US citizen, he was "not entitled . . . to sue in its courts."

The Declaration of Independence and its promise of equality had had nothing to do with "the enslaved African race," wrote Taney, given that "the conduct of the distinguished men who framed the Declaration of Independence would have been utterly and flagrantly inconsistent with the principles they asserted" were Blacks comparable, in any way, to themselves. Instead, he argued, the Framers had believed that Blacks were so inferior that "they had no rights which the white man was bound to respect."

Taney also declared the Missouri Compromise, which had maintained the balance between slave and free states, to be unconstitutional.

The decision, meant to settle the slavery issue, instead angered abolitionists and generated fuel for the antislavery cause. Northern legislators entertained proposals to free all enslaved persons brought within their states' borders. "The Slave Power will find that all extreme measures to uphold and enforce its monstrous pretensions will only react against it. Such States as Ohio, New York, and Massachusetts, containing nearly as many white people as the whole South, are not to be suppressed by Judge Taney and his antediluvian associates," thundered the the abolitionist newspaper *National Era*.

Meanwhile, numerous papers ran features about abolitionists coming together to stop arrests of Black fugitives—or of judges and other officials ridiculing Taney's logic. One defense lawyer, citing Taney's decision, argued for the release of his client on that grounds that enslaved persons, "being chattels, *not persons*, are incapable of committing crime."

Into this combustible atmosphere charged the antislavery zealot John Brown. In October 1859, Brown led a small band of followers on a raid of a federal armory in Virginia with the hope of sparking a slave insurrection. Although he and his men killed several soldiers and temporarily seized the armory and its arsenal, he was quickly captured.

After less than an hour's deliberation, the jury convicted Brown of "treason, and conspiracy and advising with slaves and others to rebel and murder in the first degree."

That November, as the apparently serene Brown awaited execution, a *New York Daily Tribune* correspondent ruminated on Brown's accomplishments: "Considered from his own point, Brown's invasion was no failure, but a vast advantage gained. I have heard him say that he believed his final triumph would be upon the scaffold, and that his assurance that his death at this time would contribute to advance the cause he has at heart, made him feel it was best for him not to encourage any of the efforts made by his friends in his behalf. . . . He has seen the frightened fury which has spread over the neighborhood of the scene of his exploit. He cannot fail to understand . . . what great events have sprung from his weak and ill-advised attempt; the entire State of Virginia blinded with madness."

The *Tribune* printed a letter Brown had written to an admirer in which he declared, "I go joyfully in behalf of millions that 'have no rights' that this great and glorious, this Christian Republic is 'bound to respect.'"

As Brown awaited execution, the *Liberator* reprinted a ballad composed in his honor by an unidentified author. "John Brown's Invasion" included such lines as "Then he grasped his trusty rifle, and boldly fought for freedom; Smote from border unto border the fierce invading band." At Brown's funeral that December, abolitionist Wendell Phillips declared, "John Brown has loosened the roots of the Slave system; it only breathes—it does not live—hereafter."

Senator Stephen Douglas blamed Republicans for John Brown's actions. In proposing a bill to protect states against invasion by inhabitants of other states, he gave a speech that, as transcribed by the *Detroit Free Press,* called John Brown's violence at Harper's Ferry "the logical, natural consequence of the teachings and doctrines of the republican party. I am not making this statement for the purpose of crimination or partisan effect. I desire to call the attention of members of that party to a reconsideration of the doctrines that they are in the habit of enforcing with a view to a fair judgment whether they do not lead directly to those consequences on the part of those deluded persons who think that all they say is meant in real earnest and ought to be carried out; The great principle that underlies the organization of the republican party is violent, irreconcilable, eternal warfare upon the institution of American slavery, with the view of its ultimate extinction throughout the land; sectional war is to be waged until the cotton fields of the South shall be cultivated by free labor, or the rye fields of New York and Massachusetts shall be cultivated by slave labor. In furtherance of this article of their creed, you find their political organization not only sectional in its location, but one whose vitality consists in appeals to northern passion, northern prejudice, northern ambition, against southern States, southern institutions, and southern people."

Democratic senator Robert Toombs of Georgia echoed Douglas, calling Republicans "enemies of the country." Abolitionists, he claimed, "have formed a coalition with all the waifs and strays—deserters of all former political parties—and the better to conceal their real purposes have assumed the name of the Republican party. This coalition has but one living, animating, principle or bond of union, and that is hatred of the people and institutions of the slaveholding States of this Union."

That view of Republicans as wild-eyed zealots was very much on Abraham Lincoln's mind when he spoke at Cooper Union in New York in February 1860. Lincoln was not yet the Republican nominee for president. Indeed, Senator William Seward of New York, widely considered to be a die-hard abolitionist, was the front-runner. In truth, Seward's position was nuanced. Although he saw an "irrepressible conflict" between slave and free states, he did not see the matter being resolved peremptorily by an imperious federal government but by "the action of the several states, cooperating with the federal government . . . in strict conformity to their respective constitutions." Lincoln sought to position himself as someone indisputably in the mainstream.

At Cooper Union, Lincoln distanced his party from John Brown, who, he pointed out, was not a Republican but "a lone individual with a plan so absurd that the slaves . . . saw plainly it could not succeed." He made clear that he had no intention of abolishing slavery in the states. Thomas Jefferson "did not mean to say, nor do I, that the power of emancipation is in the Federal Government," he declared.

He insisted, however, that the federal government had every right to prohibit expansion of slavery into the federal territories and argued that his position was identical to that of the Founders. "[Of] our thirty-nine fathers who framed the original Constitution, twenty-one—a clear majority of the whole—certainly understood that no proper division of local from federal authority, nor any part of the Constitution, forbade the

Federal Government to control slavery in the federal territories; while all the rest probably had the same understanding," he asserted.

He addressed "a few words to the Southern people," denouncing their threat to succeed as nothing less than extortion. He also criticized their adamant anti-Republicanism: "You will grant a hearing to pirates or murderers, but nothing like it to 'Black Republicans.' " He asked for an end to the reckless rhetoric, urged faith in the idea that "right makes might," and challenged the audience to "dare to do our duty as we understand it."

At the Republican National Convention in Chicago in May, Lincoln, on the third ballot, beat Seward, who had led after the first and second rounds.

"The nomination of Mr. Lincoln for the Presidency by the republican national convention has been received by the party in Illinois and the Northwest with an enthusiasm unparalleled since the days of 1840," reported the *Detroit Free Press*.

No such enthusiasm greeted the news in the South, which saw Lincoln's selection as essentially a declaration of war on its way of life. If the Black Republicans had their way, argued the *Louisville Courier Journal*, "The fugitive slave law, already nullified, will be repealed; slavery will be abolished in the District of Columbia; the Inter-State slave trade will be prohibited; and . . . our sugar and rice fields and cotton plantations will be converted into one vast desert."

Lincoln ended up in a four-way race with Southern Democrat John Breckinridge, Northern Democrat Stephen Douglas, and Constitutional Union Party candidate John Bell. Lincoln swept the North (with the exception of New Jersey) and totally lost the South (where, for the most part, he was not on the ballot). He nonetheless ended up with a plurality of the votes and a majority in the Electoral College.

The *Independent*, a progressive political journal, proclaimed his win a "GREAT TRIUMPH" and declared, "The power of the slave-interest at Washington is broken."

3

THE SOUTH SECEDES

Lincoln was not due in Washington for the inauguration until March 1861, which gave the South plenty of time for mischief. Some feared that the southern states might try to overthrow the government before he was sworn in. Instead, they opted to leave.

In December, Howell Cobb, a former congressman and governor from Georgia, resigned his position as secretary of the treasury and wrote an open letter to the citizens of Georgia all but declaring the South's intention to secede: "Can there be any doubt in any intelligent mind that the object which the Black Republican party has in view is the ultimate extinction of slavery in the United States. . . . In the nomination of Mr. Lincoln for the Presidency, the Black Republicans gave still more pointed expression of their views and feelings on the subject of slavery."

He accused Lincoln of "holding sentiments even more odious than those of Seward" and predicted that the Republican "abolitionists" would bring degradation and ruin to Georgia: "I entertain no doubt either of your right or duty to secede from the Union. Arouse, then, all your manhood for the great work before you, and be prepared . . . to announce and maintain your independence out of The Union, for you will never again have equality and justice in it."

Cobb became the head of the Provisional Congress of the Confederate States and ultimately a general in the Confederate Army.

On December 17, the *New York Times* published a letter from the wife of an officer at Fort Moultrie, South Carolina, who warned of an impending crisis: "Within a few days we hear—and from so many sources that we cannot doubt it—that the Charlestonians are erecting two batteries, one just opposite us, at a little village, Mount Pleasant, and another on the end of this island. . . . I suppose President Buchanan and Secretary [of War John] Floyd intend the Southern Confederation to be cemented with the blood of this brave little garrison."

Several days later, a *Times* correspondent reported that Fort Moultrie had been ordered to surrender if attacked: "I am reliably informed that Major Anderson telegraphed that he had surrendered a large number of arms, which had been removed from the arsenal to Fort Moultrie, to the authorities at Charleston, on a demand being made for them. This was done in obedience, so he says, to the spirit of the orders he has received from Washington."

The first state to secede was South Carolina. Its legislature convened a "secession convention" in Charleston, which passed an ordinance of secession on December 20 and confirmed it with a declaration of secession on December 24. A procession of self-styled Minutemen paraded through Charleston in celebration, accompanied by fireworks and music. "The city is alive with pleasurable excitement," reported the *Baltimore Sun*. Alabama and Florida greeted the news with hundred-gun salutes. Over the next few weeks, Mississippi, Florida, Alabama, Georgia, Louisiana, and Texas also abandoned the Union.

With the secession crisis in full flower and the press and politicians speculating about southern states seizing the nation's capital—and perhaps preventing the certification of Lincoln's electoral victory—Lincoln was preparing for a train journey from Springfield, Illinois, to Washington. He would greet dignitaries and constituents at stops in Indiana, Ohio, Pennsylvania, New York, Baltimore, and elsewhere along the way. The odyssey was scheduled to take just short of two weeks.

On the morning of February 11, well-wishers assembled at the train station to see him off. Lincoln addressed them from the platform. He acknowledged his sadness in leaving them after a quarter of a century in residence there. "To this place and the kindness of the people, I owe everything," he said. "Here my children have been born and one is buried. I now leave, not knowing when or whether I ever may return with a task before me greater than that which rested upon Washington. . . . Trusting in Him who can go with me and remain with you . . . let us confidently hope that all will yet be well."

On February 13, the counting of the electoral vote proceeded without overt threat or incident—despite fears of an armed invasion. Vice President John Breckinridge pronounced "Abraham Lincoln of Illinois" the "duly elected President of the United States for the four years, commencing on the 4th of March."

The *New York Times* observed, "To-day was one of those fixed upon for the contemplated raid on the Capital, and a few weeks ago many freely predicted that the counting of the electoral votes would never be peacefully accomplished. The day has passed remarkably calm. Even the atmosphere was soft and balmy, and the air so still that the national flags over the Capitol hung closely to their staves."

The *New York Tribune* also noted the widespread anxiety over the prospect that "bodies of armed men, with hostile intent" harbored "diabolical plans against the federal capitol." Federal troops were prepared for such an assault, which never came. Indeed, it would be 160 years before a mob of Americans actually attacked the US Capitol with the goal of stopping the transition of presidential power.

The day his victory was certified, Lincoln gave a speech in Columbus, Ohio, and expressed faith that God would solve the problems facing the nation. Several days later, he learned from Pinkerton detectives guarding him (there was not yet a Secret Service) that assassins might await him in Baltimore. Pinkerton feared that Baltimore officials, including the police chief, might somehow be involved. If Lincoln stopped in Baltimore, they thought, the plotters might strike while he was under the protection of the suspect police chief.

His protectors came up with a plan to take him, via private train, directly from Harrisburg to Washington, skipping Baltimore altogether. They executed the plan flawlessly and arrived safely in Washington around 6:00 a.m. on February 23.

When news leaked out that Lincoln had skipped Baltimore because of the supposed plot, he became an object of ridicule. The *Baltimore Sun* scoffed at the shenanigans accompanying Lincoln's arrival in Washington. Cartoonists piled on, picturing Lincoln skulking about, presumably evading assassins, in a plaid cap and military cloak.

On inauguration day, March 4, the state of the union was more perilous than ever. Numerous states had seceded, and others seemed on the verge of doing so. Rebels were demanding that Union troops vacate Fort Sumter in South Carolina, but war had not yet broken out.

The day started out cloudy. But the clouds cleared before Lincoln spoke. He acknowledged the South's anxiety but argued that it was baseless: "I have no purpose, directly or indirectly, to interfere with the institution of slavery in the States where it exists. I believe I have no lawful right to do so." The Constitution required the return "of what we call fugitive slaves," he asserted, and suggested the Constitution be obeyed.

He eschewed the use of unnecessary violence: "The power confided to me will be used to hold, occupy, and possess the property and places belonging to the Government and to collect the duties and imposts; but beyond what may be necessary for these objects, there will be no invasion, no using of force against or among the people anywhere."

Finally, he appealed for unity: "A husband and wife may be divorced and go out of the presence and beyond the reach of each other, but the different parts of our country cannot do this. . . . We must not be enemies."

The day after his inauguration, Lincoln informed Governor Francis Pickens of South Carolina that the Union would not surrender Fort Sumter. On April 12, the South Carolina militia opened fire on the fort. Major Robert Anderson, surrendered the fort, setting off the Civil War.

––––––

When the war began, Lincoln did not consider liberating those Blacks who were still in chains, but the abolitionist Frederick Douglass thought that was absurd. Why let traitors benefit from enslaved workers? As long as "the Government continues to refuse the aid of colored men," the slave states would continue to have an advantage, he argued. "Men in earnest don't fight with one hand, when they might fight with two, and a man drowning would not refuse to be saved even by a colored hand."

As the war wore on, Lincoln warmed to the idea of emancipation. But he wanted to announce the policy from a position of uncontested strength, preferably after a major military victory.

He settled for the Battle of Antietam. Fought on September 17, 1862, it was one of the bloodiest encounters of the war. By the time General Robert E. Lee was forced to retreat, an estimated 3,650 soldiers had died—with both sides taking heavy casualties, although more Union than Confederate troops died. Nonetheless, the Union declared victory. "Another Great Battle! Success of the Union Army," exclaimed the *Baltimore Sun*.

On September 22, Lincoln formally announced his plan for emancipation: on January 1, 1863, "all persons held as slaves within any states, or designated part of a state, the people whereof shall then be in rebellion against the United States shall be then, thenceforward, and forever free."

With that proclamation, the war fundamentally changed. It was no longer just a fight to restore the Union but "one to destroy the old Union and build a new one purged of human bondage," observed the historian James McPherson. Many of Lincoln's contemporaries agreed.

"By a word the President transforms a State sunk in the semi-barbarism of a medieval age to the light and civilization of the Nineteenth Christian Century," declared the *New-York Daily Tribune*.

The Union, however, was not quite ready for what that light revealed. Even though he had theoretically freed millions with the stroke of a pen, Lincoln had done nothing to provide for their safety or well-being, leaving them little choice but to continue living in bondage or risk ruin and sorrow attempting to claim their freedom from people determined to keep them in subjugation. Henry Wright, a soldier and supporter of emancipation, expressed his concerns for the welfare of the Black freemen in a letter to the *Liberator*:

[Unless] some preparation is made ere the first of January for the emancipated slaves, we shall see a reign of starvation worse than Ireland ever saw. . . . [The] colored people who escape from slavery to our lines are now dying of starvation! Scores of contrabands [escaped former slaves] daily arrive. They flock within our lines. We protect them; we render their freedom secure; but, alas! freedom cannot supply them food. So, in many instances, they die! . . . To sleep together in the streets, by hundreds, as they do, would surely kill white people.

Wright's words were prophetic. Those who had managed to escape to "freedom" continued to live in anxiety and need. A special correspondent to the *Chicago Tribune*, writing from Memphis in November

1863, observed that Union soldiers were unprepared for the flood of newly "freed" Black people who came seeking help: "At first they were sent back to their rebel masters, driven outside of our lines by our officers, and only occasionally a few of them allowed to remain in the camps as servants to the officers or cooks for soldiers' messes."

Eventually, the military organized "contraband camps," settlements in which escapees could live as they prepared for a life of independence. Reporting on a camp that housed an estimated sixteen hundred in Craney Island, Virginia, the *Boston Herald* observed that residents lived in wooden barracks or canvas tents that, to some extent, they managed themselves: "[There] are 4 contraband women and 1 contraband man in charge of each block. It is the duty of this man and these women to see that the rations are properly distributed, that the children are cared for, that there is cleanliness in and about the quarter."

In September 1863, Union Army commanding general Ulysses S. Grant visited a contraband camp near Natchez, Mississippi, "for the purpose of organizing some negro regiments," reported the *New York Times*. The *Times* observed that of the six thousand residents in the camp, "some three hundred will be fit for military service—a small proportion, indeed, but it must be remembered that the hardships and exposures of Slavery are not conducive to the health of slaves." Also, noted the *Times*, the military would need Blacks as "teamsters, cooks, Quartermaster's hands and officers' servants."

Some freemen benefited from private assistance. A group calling itself the Contraband Relief Association of Washington, founded by free Black women in 1862, focused on providing material help to those who had made it behind Union lines. In its first annual report, issued in August 1863, the association observed that "the present state of affairs existing in this country, having caused many of the hitherto oppressed people of a portion of God's race to be cast among us in a most deplorable condition, our hearts have been made to sympathize with them, and we have pledged ourselves to do all we can to alleviate their sufferings."

That help consisted largely of food, clothing, and medical assistance. "We have not accomplished as much during the last year as we had desired, yet there is satisfaction in knowing that, as we have fed the hungry, clothed the naked, and ministered to the wants of the suffering, we have been instrumental in doing some good," said the association's report.

Despite the many hardships endured by the formerly enslaved and their very limited options as newly freed men and women, Frederick Douglass focused on the positive. He "thanked God that he was living to see the beginning of the end of slavery," reported the *Globe and Mail*.

———

The Civil War ended in April 1865 with the Union victory at the Battle of Appomattox Court House and Robert E. Lee's surrender to Ulysses S. Grant. It was the bloodiest conflict in US history, costing some 620,000 American lives.

In a speech several days later, Lincoln proclaimed a National Day of Thanksgiving and expressed hope for a "righteous and speedy peace." That was Lincoln's final public address. He was shot by John Wilkes Booth on the evening of April 14, during a performance at Ford's Theatre in Washington, DC. He died shortly after seven the next morning, never having regained consciousness.

Booth was quickly identified as the assassin. The killing was part of a plot that also unsuccessfully targeted Secretary of State William Seward and Vice President Andrew Johnson. Booth, who had suffered a broken leg while fleeing from Ford's Theatre, was shot and killed by pursuing militia on the morning of April 26.

In a letter left with his brother-in-law, Booth explained his motivation. He saw Lincoln's election as a declaration of war "upon Southern rights and institutions," which threatened to elevate Blacks beyond their station. "This country was formed for the white man, not the black man." No one "would be willing to do more for the negro race than I," he asserted, but eliminating slavery, he said, would help neither Blacks nor Whites. Slavery was "one of the greatest blessings (both for themselves and us) that God ever bestowed upon a favored nation," whereas the policies of Lincoln and his fellow abolitionists, which were dragging America "deeper and deeper into cruelty and oppression," would ruin Blacks and Whites alike.

Abraham Lincoln's death left the United States under the care of Andrew Johnson. A Democrat and former senator and governor from Tennessee, Johnson had served as military governor of his home state before Lincoln had made him his running mate on a ticket meant to symbolize national unity.

Johnson had shown up drunk for his inauguration as vice president, reeling from an overdose of whiskey consumed to aid his recovery from a hangover and typhoid fever. The press skewered him. "Andrew Johnson . . . dragged [America's] proudest ceremony into the slough of his degradation and turned it to shame and humiliation," groused the *Pittsburgh Gazette*. "We hold that if a public man is drunken . . . while acting his part on a public occasion, his offense is against the public" and merits "public censure," commented the *New York Independent*. The *Cincinnati Daily Enquirer* called Johnson a "national disgrace."

After Lincoln died, the press became more forgiving of Johnson, whom some abolitionists suddenly saw as the best hope for an honorable peace. As someone who had been born poor and White in the South, Johnson "knows how and why his class are kept down there," observed the *New-York Daily Tribune*, adding "of all anti-Slavery men we have found these the most radical and inflexible." The *Tribune* thought it inconceivable that Johnson would "leave a vestige of Slavery on the continent." Indeed, after Johnson denounced rebel "traitors" and suggested that "evildoers" might be punished, some progressives wondered whether he might be tougher on unrepentant rebels than Lincoln had been.

4

A TASTE OF FREEDOM BEFORE RE-ENSLAVEMENT

In his State of the Union address the December before his death, Lincoln had urged the House, during its lame-duck session, to approve a constitutional amendment abolishing slavery. The Senate had already passed the measure. Lincoln suggested that it was "only a question of time" before the House did as well, especially since the incoming House would be dominated by Republicans. The House accepted the president's reasoning and moved forward. It was Lincoln's last major victory. Upon his elevation to the presidency, Johnson took up the mantle, supporting the amendment's ratification.

In his first State of the Union address in December 1865, Johnson declared that it was "not too much to ask" states rejoining the Union to support "the abolition of slavery forever within the limits of our country. So long as the adoption of this amendment is delayed, so long will doubt and jealousy and uncertainty prevail."

He made clear that he would take things only so far. He was not demanding that Blacks get the vote. That decision, he argued, should be made by each state. Nothing in the Constitution or law, he said, supported the president pushing such a proposition.

Many liberals had assumed that Johnson's experience as a poor southerner had rendered him sympathetic to the formerly enslaved. They also thought that his background gave him useful insights into the White southern mind. "It was widely believed that Andrew Johnson held more radical ideas on reconstruction than Lincoln. Johnson seemingly confirmed this belief by his thundering denunciations of traitors during the week after the assassination. 'Mr. Lincoln's too great kindness of heart led him to a mistaken leniency,' wrote William Lloyd Garrison, Jr., 'but Andy Johnson has fought the beasts of Ephesus on their own soil and has learned by bitter experience their implacable nature,' " observed James McPherson, in *The Struggle for Equality: Abolitionists and the Negro in the Civil War and Reconstruction*.

Michael Burlingame, author of *Abraham Lincoln: A Life,* made much the same point: "Within hours of learning that Lincoln had died, Henry Ward Beecher declared: 'Johnson's little finger was stronger than Lincoln's loins.' A Presbyterian minister in Freeport, Illinois, asserted that Lincoln 'had fulfilled the purpose for which God had raised him up, and he passed off the stage because some different instrument was needed for the full accomplishment of the Divine purpose in the affairs of our nation.' "

The liberal optimists failed to see that Johnson was a die-hard racist—implacably opposed to the very idea of Black equality. Johnson's private secretary "once wrote in his diary that Johnson 'exhibited a morbid distress and feeling against the negroes,' McPherson noted. "During the war a friend in Tennessee reminded Johnson that the abolitionists hoped to make free citizens out of the slaves. 'Damn the negroes,' replied Johnson. 'I am fighting these traitorous aristocrats, their masters.' "

As president, in matters involving the formerly enslaved, Johnson generally deferred to the very individuals who had fought a war to keep them in bondage.

Before former Confederate states could be readmitted to the Union, Johnson required them to agree to emancipation, swear loyalty to the United States, and ratify the Thirteenth Amendment. He did not demand that Blacks be treated with dignity, although he counseled against their "forced removal."

The states responded by passing an array of laws ("Black codes") crafted to keep Blacks in subjugation—although many of the laws did not explicitly identify Blacks as their target.

With the exceptions of Arkansas and Tennessee, every southern state outlawed vagrancy, "so vaguely defining it that virtually any freed slave not under the protection of a white man could be arrested for the crime," wrote the journalist Douglas Blackmon in *Slavery by Another Name: The Re-enslavement of Black Americans from the Civil War to World War II*. Mississippi, he noted, "required African American workers to enter into labor contracts with white farmers by January 1 of every year or risk arrest." Other states made it illegal to hire Blacks who lacked a discharge paper from their previous employer.

States also passed laws effectively re-enslaving Blacks who had been convicted of crimes. In a society in which Blacks were barred from juries and not allowed to vote, African Americans were routinely convicted on little more than a White person's word. The system, abusive on its face, also bred corruption. Blackmon tells the story of Alabama governor Robert M. Patton, who, for five dollars total, leased 374 state prisoners to an enterprise controlled by the Alabama and Chattanooga Railroad, of which Patton soon after became president. Such cozily corrupt agreements were routine.

The result was a South still steeped in White supremacy, a "sham democracy," in the words of the *New-York Tribune*. Peter Alfred Taylor, an English member of Parliament, was so astounded by the situation in the United States that he wrote a letter to the *Liberator* questioning whether slavery had actually been abolished. He pointed out that Negroes were still "tied hand and foot at the disposition of laws made exclusively by . . . masters" who despised them.

Many northern states also had "Black laws." Under the laws in effect in Illinois, Blacks in the state were presumed to be runaway slaves unless they could prove otherwise. Those lacking proper credentials could be jailed for six weeks. If they failed to produce the required documents, they could be hired out for a year for the benefit of the county. Black servants found more than ten miles from home without a pass could be punished with thirty-five lashes. Even Blacks entering the state with proper identification were required to post a $1,000 bond to ensure that they would not become a burden. In 1865, feeling pressure to show more tolerance, the state repealed its Black laws except for the prohibition against interracial marriage.

The North also routinely denied Black residents the right to vote, which the Democratic press in the South loved to point out.

Restitution was another charged issue. After being forced to give former slaves their freedom, southerners were generally disinclined to give Blacks anything else. But many Blacks—and their advocates—felt that a debt was owed them, that the formerly enslaved deserved at least enough assistance to enable them to start life anew. Indeed, Union general William T. Sherman had raised expectations with his Special Field Order No. 15.

The order had come at the end of Sherman's victorious "March to the Sea," which had come to resemble a scene from Exodus. Multitudes of escaped Blacks had followed Sherman's soldiers as they had advanced through Georgia, vanquishing the Confederate forces. Atlanta had fallen in September 1864, and Savannah had succumbed in December.

On January 12, 1865, General Sherman and Secretary of War

Edwin Stanton met with twenty "freedmen" at Sherman's Savannah headquarters. The freedmen chose Garrison Frazier, a native of Granville County, North Carolina, and an ordained Baptist minister, as their spokesman. The sixty-seven-year-old Frazier had purchased freedom for himself and his wife for $1,000 in gold and silver eight years prior to the meeting.

Asked to explain the presidential proclamation of emancipation, Frazier replied, "The freedom as I understand it . . . is taking us from under the yoke of bondage and placing us where we could reap the fruit of our own labor, take care of ourselves, and assist the Government in maintaining our freedom." The "way we can best take care of ourselves," he added, was to be given land to till "by our own labor." In a separate conversation with Secretary Stanton, Frazier suggested that land given to freedmen should be away from Whites and the prejudice they harbored, which would "take years to get over."

Stanton later remarked that the meeting was the first time the government had directly asked those "poor debated people . . . what they wanted for themselves."

Four days later, Sherman issued the special field order: "The islands from Charleston, south, the abandoned rice fields along the rivers for thirty miles back from the sea, and the country bordering the St. Johns river, Florida, are reserved and set apart for the settlement of the negroes now made free by the acts of war and the proclamation of the President of the United States." Altogether, he designated an estimated 400,000 acres of land—a maximum of 40 acres per family—and prohibited Whites from occupying it, with the exception of military officials.

His order encouraged Black men to enlist in the army by allowing "a negro [who] has enlisted in the military service . . . [to] locate his family in any one of the settlements at pleasure, and acquire a homestead, and all other rights and privileges of a settler, as though present in person."

The order effectively promised permanent resettlement for some 40,000 Blacks, but, as the historian Barton Myers pointed out, the promise was not kept: "Despite the objections of General Oliver O. Howard, the Freedmen's Bureau chief, US president Andrew Johnson overturned Sherman's directive in the fall of 1865, after the war had ended, and returned most of the land . . . to the planters who had originally owned it."

Many historians believe Sherman's order to be the origin of the belief that Blacks, after the Civil War, were promised forty acres and a mule. Had Sherman's commitment been kept and expanded upon—as the congressionally created Bureau of Refugees, Freedmen, and Abandoned Lands envisioned—America's post–Civil War experience would have been fundamentally different. The New South would have been forced to adjust to the presence of independent Blacks. But in a blink, that possibility vanished as the US government deemed restoring property to traitors to the Union more important than giving formerly enslaved people a fighting chance.

———

Andrew Johnson delivered his first annual message to Congress on December 4, 1865, two days before the Thirteenth Amendment was ratified. He shared his view that the federal government had done enough for the freedmen. The rest was up to the leaders of the former Confederate states. "When the tumult of emotions that have been raised by the suddenness of the social change shall have subsided," he opined, the freedmen might "receive the kindest usage from some of those on whom they have heretofore most closely depended." Johnson was essentially announcing his intention to take an ax to the Republican agenda.

When Congress moved to renew the extension of the Freedman's Bureau in 1866, Johnson vetoed it, arguing that "military jurisdiction" over the South discriminated against Whites. Johnson also vetoed the

Civil Rights Act of 1866, which granted citizenship to all males born in the United States "without distinction of race or color, or previous condition of slavery or involuntary servitude."

In his veto message that March, Johnson accused Congress of establishing safeguards "for the security of the colored race . . . which go indefinitely beyond any that the General Government has ever provided for the white race." He questioned whether it was "sound policy to make our entire colored population and all other excepted classes citizens of the United States. Four million of them have just emerged from slavery. . . . Can it be reasonably supposed that they possess the requisite qualifications . . . ?"

Congress approved the law over his veto that April. "The scene in the House, when it passed by more than a two-thirds vote . . . was one of tumultuous joy; the galleries applauded vociferously," reported the *Independent*. That July, Congress passed (and overrode Johnson's veto of) the new Freedmen's Bureau extension act.

Conflict between Johnson and the Republicans only increased after the 1866 midterm elections, which the Republicans won in a landslide. In March 1867, Congress passed the Reconstruction Act of 1867— again over Johnson's veto. The act divided the South into five military districts, each under the control of a former Union general. In order for states to be readmitted to the Union, they were required to extend suffrage to Blacks and to ratify what would become the Fourteenth Amendment, providing for citizenship, equal protection, and due process to all within the jurisdiction of the United States.

————

Johnson's relationship with Congress reached its nadir in February 1868 after the president dismissed Secretary of War Edwin Stanton, who opposed his anti-Reconstruction policies. The House concluded that the firing (without the Senate's permission) violated the newly passed

Tenure of Office Act and voted to impeach him. Johnson's trial in the Senate began on March 5 and ended on May 16. The vote, thirty-five voting guilty and nineteen for exoneration, was one short of the two-thirds majority required for removal from office. Seven Republican senators voted against the conviction, leading to widespread suspicion that they had been bribed.

The Republican Party unanimously chose war hero Ulysses S. Grant as its presidential nominee. The Democratic Party declined to support Johnson for a second term—although he "clung to the notion, to the last, that he might be nominated," according to the *New York Tribune*. Instead, on the twenty-second ballot, Democrats nominated former New York governor Horatio Seymour by acclamation. Seymour's name had been put forth by George Pendleton, the Democratic vice presidential nominee of 1864 and a presidential aspirant for 1868. "Let us vote for a man whom the Presidency has sought and who has not sought the Presidency," he exhorted after withdrawing his own name.

The election was a referendum on Reconstruction. The Republican platform, which praised Congress's "reconstruction projects," called for "equal civil and political rights for all" and demanded "equal suffrage to all loyal men" of the South. The Democrats demanded amnesty for Confederate rebels, immediate restoration of "all the States to their rights in the Union," and the abolition of all efforts and institutions designed to "secure negro supremacy."

Grant won 53 percent of the popular vote and more than doubled Seymour's electoral vote total: 214 to 80. The abolitionist publisher Horace Greeley claimed that Grant's margin would have been even larger if the southern states had not driven "loyal blacks from the polls" or compelled them "by the terrors of massacres and famine, to vote for their oppressors." Republicans retained control of both houses of Congress.

The *Atlanta Constitution* warned radical Republicans about reading too much into their electoral victory, attributing it largely to Grant's personal popularity. The election was therefore not "an indorsement by the people of the extreme measures and programme of the ruling Radicals of the present Congress." The Republicans disagreed.

In February 1869, Congress approved the Fifteenth Amendment, which eliminated "race, color, or previous condition of servitude" as barriers to the right to vote. It was ratified in February 1870. The *Cincinnati Daily Enquirer*, reflecting an attitude typical of the Democratic press, grumbled that "mongrel gangs of negroes and other chicken-thieves . . . under bayonet coercion" had forced the amendment on the southern states.

—————

Despite the outrage at the concessions to Blacks among White southerners and their allies, freedmen were eager for change. In August 1865, the *New York Times* published an emotional plea from "The Late Convention of Colored Men" addressed "to the loyal citizens of the United States and to Congress":

> When the contest waxed long, and the result hung doubtfully, you appealed to us for help, and how well we answered. . . .
>
> Well, the war is over, the rebellion is "put down," and we are declared, free! Four-fifths of our enemies are paroled or amnestied, and the other fifth are being pardoned, and the President has . . . left us entirely at the mercy of these subjugated but unconverted rebels, in everything save the privilege of bringing us, our wives and little ones, to the auction block. . . . [In] the hour of your peril you called upon us, and . . . we came at your call and you are saved; and now we beg, we pray, we entreat you not to desert us in this the hour of our peril!

And indeed the Union did not desert them—at least not right away.

Although Reconstruction brought White southerners misery, it lifted Blacks—ever so tenuously—out of Hell. For the first time, Blacks in the South became something other than victims. Some even became members of Congress.

"Between 1869 and 1875 sixteen blacks from seven Southern states served in Congress, six from South Carolina, three each from Alabama and Mississippi. Florida, Louisiana, Georgia and North Carolina each elected one black Congressman. Naturally, all were Republicans," observed John Hosmer and Joseph Fineman in the journal *Phylon*. By one count, the total number of Black public officials during that era was more than fifteen hundred. Louisiana even briefly had a Black governor. P.B.S. Pinchback, whose father was White, served just over a month, from December 9, 1872, to January 13, 1873.

Pinchback was not elected to that office. He had been chosen as president pro tempore of the state senate and, under state rules, was elevated to the office of acting lieutenant governor after lieutenant governor Oscar Dunn, also a Black man, died in November 1871. Shortly after that, Governor Henry Warmoth became embroiled in impeachment proceedings against him and Pinchback became acting governor.

An indignant district judge, calling Pinchbeck a "naked trespasser," ordered him to be physically removed from office. Backed up by deputy marshals, Pinchback refused to step aside. Instead, he dissolved the court.

Such power in the hands of Blacks was not something the South would long abide. Whites rose up in anger. The so-called Memphis massacre erupted in May 1866 following a flare-up between Black veterans and White policemen. Forty-six Blacks were killed and many more raped, injured, or robbed. That July, in New Orleans, scores of Blacks were butchered for protesting the passage of so-called Black codes.

White grievance eventually spawned the Ku Klux Klan. Historians believe that the KKK originated in Pulaski, Tennessee, in late 1865. Its popularity quickly grew, and it became the deadliest "domestic terrorist movement in the history of the United States," wrote Elaine Frantz Parsons, in *Ku-Klux: The Birth of the Klan During Reconstruction*. From 1866 to 1871, reported Parsons, the Klan "killed hundreds of black southerners and their white supporters, sexually molested hundreds of black women and men, drove thousands of black families from their homes and thousands of black men and women from their employment, and appropriated land, crops, guns, livestock, and food from black southerners on a massive scale."

For many Whites, the Klan was a source of pride. It saw itself not as a vile hate group but as a "protective organization." "We are not the enemy of the blacks as long as they behave themselves," declared a KKK manifesto delivered to the *Republican Banner,* a Nashville-based newspaper, in 1868. The problem, reasoned the manifesto's authors, was with Black belligerence that forced Whites "to hostilities."

For southern White males, support of the Klan became almost obligatory. And they justified joining by insisting that the Klan was "an institution of Chivalry, Humanity, Mercy and Patriotism," in the words of F. Michael Higginbotham, the author of *Ghosts of Jim Crow: Ending Racism in Post-racial America.*

A Senate select committee disagreed. The Select Committee of the Senate to Investigate Alleged Outrages in the Southern States published a report in January 1871 that included several interviews with KKK members. James Boyd of North Carolina admitted that he had joined the White Brotherhood (another name for the KKK) in 1868. The mission was "the overthrow of the reconstruction policy of Congress and disfranchisement of the negro"—even, he acknowledged, if people had to be killed to bring that about. Other witnesses admitted that scores of Black men, women, and children had been shot, whipped, robbed, hung, and drowned with impunity. "In nine cases out of ten, the men who commit the crimes constitute or sit on the grand jury, either they themselves, or their near relatives or friends, sympathizers, aiders, or abettors," explained a southern judge. He added that he had "heard of no instance" in his state of Klansmen being convicted for their crimes.

In March 1871, President Grant sent Congress a message bemoaning conditions in the South that rendered "life and property insecure and the carrying of the mails and the collection of the revenue dangerous." State authorities, he declared, were powerless to "correct these evils" and he therefore recommended legislation to "secure life, liberty, and property, and the enforcement of law."

Congress had already passed one Enforcement Act in 1870 that prohibited discrimination and violence against Black voters and another in February 1871 that put the federal government and its military in charge of polling places during national elections. In April, it passed a third Enforcement Act. The legislation, also known as the Ku Klux Klan Act, outlawed many Klan tactics and empowered the president to use the militia and take other measures to crush the Klan. The bill provided for certain offenses to be tried in federal courts, for the swearing in of jurors who were not Klan sympathizers, and for cracking down on those who refused to reveal knowledge of the Klan's violent plans as accessories before the fact.

The strong federal role was deemed necessary because the Klan had totally co-opted local officials. Grant's tough approach, though effective in reducing violence, also provoked a backlash—and not just among southerners but among northerners who rejected any notion of racial equality and openly questioned whether an effort aimed at protecting and improving Black lives was worth the trouble.

A number of Democratic newspapers routinely minimized the threat from the Klan or denied its existence altogether. Some blamed the violence on Blacks who, in their telling and for some mysterious reason, had taken to wearing disguises and randomly attacking Whites. Those anti-Black editors wholeheartedly agreed with the Select Senate Committee minority report that assailed "measures taken to array the negroes" who were "against the white people" and were assisted by "carpet-bag allies, backed by the military power of the Government."

In April 1871, the *Atlanta Constitution* printed a letter from a self-confessed KKK member who claimed he was aware of only one case in which the Klan had driven a Black person out of town. And that had been the result of a prank. A Ku Kluxer disguised as a ghost of the "negro's departed great grandfather" had frightened the gullible Negro, who had bolted in terror.

In May 1871, the *Cincinnati Enquirer* ran a story, "How the Ku-Klux Outrages are Manufactured," suggesting that the Klan was wrongly accused of committing murders and creating mayhem. That June, the *Detroit Free Press* reported on an Alabama judge who "said he did not believe any such organization as the Ku-Klux existed in Alabama." The comment was made in testimony before the Joint Select Committee to Inquire into the Condition of Affairs in the Late Insurrectionary States (otherwise known as the Southern Outrage Committee). The newspaper followed that up with an article in which a Georgia official denied any Klan presence in his state, although he admitted that some "mischievous young men" had "wrapped themselves in sheets and scared superstitious negroes." The only crime he could recall being committed had been by Blacks: "Three negroes had disguised themselves and whipped a white man in Clark County." Another group of disguised Negroes had "attempted the murder of a white man named Hancock."

Such Klan-friendly propaganda, along with overwhelming support for the Klan in the South, was one reason that Grant's fight against racist terrorism and violence was doomed.

In his State of the Union address in December 1874, Grant voiced his frustration at the southern states' continued "acts of violence and intimidation" committed to deny Blacks access to ballots: "Bands of men, masked and armed, made their appearance; White Leagues and other societies were formed; large quantities of arms and ammunition were imported and distributed to these organizations; military drills, with menacing demonstrations, were held; and, with all these, murders enough were committed to spread terror among those whose political action was to be suppressed."

In such an environment, he noted, "the whole scheme of colored enfranchisement is worse than mockery, and little better than a crime." He went on to call for "fairness in the discussion of southern questions" and pointed out, "Under existing conditions, the negro votes the republican ticket because he knows his friends are of that party. . . . Treat the negro as a citizen and a voter—as he is and must remain—and soon parties will be divided, not on the color line, but on principle. Then we shall have no complaint of sectional interference."

Democrats did not take his advice. The violence and political pushback continued. Grant left office in disappointment. As the historian Brooks Simpson put it, "Grant reluctantly conceded that his policy of conciliation had failed 'because it was all on one side. . . . I do not see what the North can do that has not been done unless we surrender the results of the war.' "

———

With the midterm elections of 1874, the dream of radical Reconstruction and racial reconciliation began to crumble. The US was reeling from the international economic crisis triggered by the collapse in 1873 of Jay Cooke & Company, the financial powerhouse behind the Northern Pacific Railway. It was also suffering from Reconstruction fatigue and had just come through the so-called Salary Grab Act scandal, which had seen Congress award huge salary increases to the president, Supreme Court justices, and other government officials just before President's Grant's second inauguration in 1873. Public outrage led Congress to rescind many of the raises in early 1874—but the damage had been done. Frustrated by the economic crisis and apparent government corruption, voters gave Democrats control of the House and sharply reduced the Republican advantage in the Senate.

In 1875, yet another scandal, the "Whiskey Ring" debacle, roiled the nation. A cabal of corrupt officials and businessmen was implicated in a scheme to divert taxes imposed on whiskey production. Some 238 individuals were indicted. Nearly half (110) were convicted. General Orville Babcock, Grant's private secretary, was among the indicted, although he was found innocent largely because of testimony Grant provided in his defense. In May 1875, Grant announced that he was not seeking a third term.

The Democrat-controlled House commended Grant's decision with a resolution on December 15 declaring, by a vote of 232 to 18, that George Washington had had the right idea in retiring from office after his second term: "the precedent . . . has become, by universal concurrence, a part of our republican system of government." To depart from that custom, it said, "would be unwise, unpatriotic, and fraught with peril to our free institutions."

The 1876 election pitted Democratic New York governor Samuel Tilden against Rutherford B. Hayes, a Republican former governor of Ohio.

The Republican platform proclaimed the party's fidelity to the principles that had "purged" the land of slavery. Until the words "all men are created equal" were "cheerfully obeyed or, if needed to be, vigorously enforced, the work of the republican party is unfinished," declared the platform.

The Democratic platform called for salvation from "corrupt centralism," which had facilitated "carpet-bag tyrannies." It also denounced "the policy which discards the liberty-loving German and tolerates the revival of the coolie trade."

Tilden, the Democrat, won the popular vote 4,288,546 to 4,034,311 and seemed poised for a victory in the Electoral College, although disputed votes in several states delayed the official total. Nonetheless, on November 8, the day after the vote, the *New York Tribune* announced, "Tilden Elected: His Electoral Majority Small." The next day's headline was less positive: "Hayes Possibly Elected: The Result Dependent on Florida and North Carolina." A day later, the *Tribune* remained unsure of who had won. "Hayes Probably President: His Election Practically Assured," declared the *Tribune*, which explained that vote totals were still in question in several states.

Electoral College members met on December 6 but were unable to designate a winner. News reports alluded to bribes as high as $10,000 being offered to electors to vote for Tilden.

The *Baltimore Sun*, relying on reports from informants in Interior Secretary Zachariah Chandler's office, surmised that "intelligence was . . . sufficient to warrant the claim that Hayes had received 185 votes, and therefore the republicans are now claiming that Hayes's election is assured." On the other hand, "Prominent democrats profess to feel satisfied that it will come out all right in the end, and the opinion now seems to be that the end will most probably be the election of Tilden by the House."

Tilden seemed to have 184 solid electoral votes, which meant he needed only 1 of the 20 electoral votes in contention to emerge victorious. Louisiana, South Carolina, and Florida collectively had 19 of those votes. Oregon, where officials had declared an elector ineligible, had 1.

Congress opted to resolve the crisis by appointing a fifteen-member special commission to oversee the electoral vote tally. Five members apiece came from the Senate, the House, and the Supreme Court. Eight members were Republicans, and seven were Democrats.

After months of machinations—and amid threats of a prolonged filibuster that would eventually leave the presidential choice in the hands of the Democrat-controlled House—Hayes was awarded all the contested votes and Congress duly announced the result.

As the historian Karen Guenther put it, "An ominous political crisis was averted when Republican concessions and promises persuaded southern Democrats to accept the commission's decision for Hayes, which ended the filibuster." The deal, however, came at a price. Republicans agreed "to withdraw federal troops from the South, to leave the state governments in the control of the conservatives, and to appoint a southern Democrat to Hayes's cabinet."

The *New-York Tribune* reported the outcome on March 2: "At 4:10 a. m. today the President of the Senate declared that Rutherford B. Hayes was elected President of the United States, and William A. Wheeler Vice-President. Congress devoted the whole day yesterday and a large part of the night to the electoral proceedings."

The *Tribune* described the night as one of "insane excitement in the House." Despite vigorous protests, the speaker had called for an anti-filibuster vote. "This was watched with great anxiety. . . . At the close the obstructionists were beaten by a bare two-thirds majority. Their whole crowd was enraged and desperate, but under the firm stand of the Speaker they were soon driven to the wall."

The *Cincinnati Enquirer* called the result "the Great Fraud." The *Fort Wayne* (Indiana) *Sentinel* grumbled, "A party with a majority of more than a quarter of a million of the popular vote, and of twenty-three in the Electoral College, which allows the defeated party to openly steal the Presidency, is certainly a failure." The *St. Louis Times* asked of Hayes, "Does he now propose to take possession of an office that has been stolen from its rightful owner, and occupy it?"

Hayes delivered in full on his side of the bargain. He effectively turned the South over to the very Whites who had enabled the KKK even while denying its existence, and they quickly stripped Blacks of all privileges and power. What the South had lost by seceding and losing the war, it won back through the Compromise of 1877.

In *The Presidents and the Constitution: A Living History*, the historian Michael A. Ross suggested that, by the time of the compromise, Reconstruction may have already been effectively dead. Perhaps "in agreeing to end Reconstruction, Hayes did not lose anything that was not already lost. By 1876, 'Redeemers' had restored white Democratic rule in all but three Southern states. In the others, Republican regimes were barely hanging on, controlling only small areas around their statehouses," he argued. Also, Democrats, who controlled the House, were pushing for the troops to go home, and northerners had lost their appetite for the fight: "So the question, Hayes's defenders maintained, was not whether to withdraw most of the troops, but when."

It's impossible to know what Hayes would have done had he won the election cleanly and had no need to mollify a Democratic House. It's equally impossible to dismiss Ross's speculation that—with northern White support waning and an unrepentant White South more assertive—Reconstruction's moment might have passed, assuming that it had ever truly existed. What is clear is that after less than a decade of serious work on racial equality, the nation decided to give up and double down on racism and the cruelty required to reinforce it.

Indeed, as the Democratic press made clear, even in relatively enlightened sectors of the North there was only so much of an appetite for the creation of an America in which Blacks would routinely sit on juries, hold high office, direct schools, launch companies, and become full partners in the American experiment. So the country put off, by nearly a century, the inevitable racial reckoning that would eventually ignite the civil rights movement.

That delay gave the United States an additional century to refine and strengthen a racial caste system. It made murder, humiliation, and disenfranchisement of Blacks routine—especially in the South. It allowed segregation in housing and discrimination in employment to become an accepted part of American life. And it left Blacks with absolutely no one to appeal to for justice when their property was stolen and their human rights were violated.

After the Compromise of 1877, the South and its sympathizers aggressively rewrote history. They made legends out of traitors and villains out of innocent—even selflessly heroic—Blacks. A pivotal date in that process was October 12, 1870, the day Confederate general Robert E. Lee died.

As Caroline E. Janney noted in *Remembering the Civil War: Reunion and the Limits of Reconciliation*, "News of his death unleashed a deep wave of mourning throughout the South not experienced since the surrender at Appomattox. . . . Confederate veterans saw Lee's death as the first real opportunity to glorify their war effort and honor their own martial spirit—to breathe new life into the Lost Cause."

They also saw it as a perfect opportunity to reimagine and recreate the battle to save slavery. The Civil War became a conflict in which White southerners were heroes whose only sin was loving the South and its Christian, God-fearing way of life.

That strategy, argued the historian John A. Simpson, created a mystique of "chivalric Southern soldiers" and their noble Confederate leaders. Indeed, "The 'moral magnificence' of Confederate leadership evolved as the single most important aspect of Southern vindication."

In this telling, race-based slavery was not just part of a noble southern tradition, it was blessed by God.

The historian Charles Reagan Wilson argued that southern civil religion "actually emerged from the Civil War experience." Southerners understood that their history, because of secession and the Civil War, was quite distinct from that of northerners, and they "thus focused the mythic, ritualistic, and organizational dimensions of their civil religion around the Confederacy," he wrote.

In that all-encompassing rewrite of history, brilliantly brought to life in 1915 in D. W. Griffith's critically acclaimed film *Birth of a Nation*, the only thing standing between piety and faithlessness, between civilization and chaos, was the magnificent Ku Klux Klan. Such epic mythmaking assuaged any possible guilt for the sin of slavery—and made it easy for America to become a place in which bigotry was seen as virtue.

5

A SUPERPOWER BURDENED WITH APARTHEID

Before World War I, the United States had no ambition to become the world's preeminent superpower. Indeed, President Woodrow Wilson had run for reelection in 1916 on an essentially isolationist motto: "He kept us out of war."

Most Americans and many Europeans were comfortable with Wilson's neutrality and with his assumption that the United States' interest would be better served not by becoming a combatant but by brokering the peace.

Germany, however, had other ideas. It refused to honor its pledge to spare US ships from submarine attacks. Also, as British intelligence discovered, Germany was proposing a secret alliance with Mexico: Germany would support Mexico's ambition to annex territory in New

Mexico, Texas, and Arizona provided that Mexico would stand with Germany if the United States entered the war.

The story became front-page news in March 1917, giving the United States little choice but to engage. On April 6, President Wilson's war resolution passed Congress overwhelmingly. Americans, for the most part, responded with cheers. War became the country's consuming enterprise.

In November 1918, Germany surrendered. The *Louisville Courier Journal* called the German surrender the "Greatest and Bloodiest Drama of World History." Other newspapers were equally ecstatic. "We are proud, immensely proud, of the fact that the establishment of American ideals had been made the primary purpose of the war, and that they are to be the essential principles of peace," editorialized the *St. Louis Globe Democrat*.

President Wilson had taken a stab at identifying those ideals in an address to Congress in April 1917 in which he had promoted "humane practices" among civilized nations. The future, as he saw it, would be defined by an unambiguously moral agenda. And the United States was suddenly awash in resources with which to take on the task. As the historian Volker Berghahn has observed, the United States was the one major nation that emerged from the war with its stature enhanced and with a significantly stronger economy. It had gone from being a debtor nation to "a creditor nation that had financed the British and French war effort against the Central Powers." It had also contributed troops and other resources that had turned the tide in favor of the Allies. Suddenly, the United States was a bona fide superpower facing countless decisions about what kind of superpower it was going to be.

Wilson acknowledged the United States' special status in July 1919 in a speech to the Senate following the signing of the Versailles Peace Treaty with Germany. The United States, he observed, "entered the war upon a different footing from every other nation except associates on this side of the sea. We entered it . . . as the disinterested champions of right and we interested ourselves in the terms of peace in no other capacity. . . . America shall, in truth, show the way. The light streams upon the path ahead."

Wilson immediately got pushback from the Senate, where many Republicans opposed participation in the League of Nations (called for in the treaty) and the "entangling alliances" to which it might commit the United States.

As the dispute played out in Congress, domestic drama seized the headlines. Indeed, even before the war ended, there were signs of trouble at home that might complicate being anointed the international champion "of right."

A riot in East St. Louis, Illinois, in 1917 had foreshadowed the unpleasantness to come. Whites were already upset that Blacks had been hired that February to replace striking Whites at the Aluminum Ore Company. But what set off the violence was rumors in May that an armed Black man had attempted to rob a White man. White mobs avenged the alleged crime by attacking and beating Blacks at random. On July 2, a second and more deadly riot broke out after Blacks reportedly opened fire on detectives they mistook for a group of White "joyriders" who had opened fire on Black homes. A full-fledged race riot ensued.

The *Atlanta Constitution* reported that White mobs had burned 310 homes, killed 28 Negroes, injured 75 more, and forced untold numbers to flee. The paper chronicled a two-day-long siege during which a "community of 80,000 persons [was] terrorized" as cops and guardsmen stood by, refusing to stop the slaughter.

At one point three Whites came upon a Black lying in a gutter, apparently dead. One of them flashed a light in his face and saw that he still breathed. "'Well, what do you know about that!' he exclaimed; 'not dead yet.' He and one of his comrades then drew their pistols and fired a bullet into the negro's head," reported the *Constitution*.

The *Los Angeles Times* reported, "Practically all of the dead and injured are negroes, who, being outnumbered at every corner, were hunted like wild animals and had little chance to retaliate on the mob of whites . . . that swarmed into the 'Black Belt' with torches, guns and ropes. The police looked on, either timidly or sympathetically; the National Guardsmen, hurried out after a singularly long delay, allowed, with nothing more than a perfunctory protest, the mob to take its vicious course; and the negroes, women and children and men, tumbled from their burning homes and frantically made their way across the river to St. Louis . . . where at present much more of law is upheld and order maintained."

"It is not without a certain irony that, at the very moment when this country is entering the war to 'make the world safe for democracy,' a riot of unexampled brutality should take place in East St. Louis, Illinois," observed *Current Opinion* magazine in August 1917. The article featured a William Charles Morris cartoon of two Black children clinging to their mother, who knelt before President Wilson. "Mr. President, why not make America safe for democracy?" read the caption.

In a speech in Carnegie Hall honoring the visiting Russian Commission, Theodore Roosevelt referenced the violence in East St. Louis. "Before we speak of justice for others, it behooves us to do justice within our own household," declared the ex-president, who compared "the murder of women and children in our own country" to anti-Jewish pogroms in the former Russian Empire.

The only person held responsible for the mayhem in East St. Louis was an apparently innocent Black dentist—who received a life sentence for killing a White policeman. In reporting on Dr. Leroy Bundy's conviction in April 1919, the *Chicago Defender* pointed out that exculpatory evidence had never been heard: "The defense was ready to introduce witnesses to testify that the riots were begun by white men; that witnesses had seen an automobile filled with white men going through the riot district firing from both sides of the car into the homes of our people . . . ; that the so-called first riot, which occurred May 28, 1917, when white men were beating our men, was the foundation of the race riot of July 1, 1917; but the efforts of the attorneys for the defense were in vain, for Judge Gilham refused to allow the jury to be told any of these facts."

The trial kicked off a year of racial violence.

"In the United States, many people—including black families with returning soldiers—fervently hoped 1919 would usher in a new epoch of peace, prosperity, and freedom. Black soldiers and workers believed their participation in the effort to make the world safe for democracy had earned them the equal rights they had been promised in the Constitution since the close of the Civil War," wrote Cameron McWhirter in *Red Summer: The Summer of 1919 and the Awakening of Black America*. Instead, they came home to "the worst spate of race riots and lynchings in American history. . . . In almost every case, white mobs . . . initiated the violence."

———

In May 1919, Charleston exploded after a group of White sailors became angry. Some accounts blamed a gambling dispute. For whatever reason, the sailors began attacking Blacks on the street. The conflict quickly spread, drawing an estimated two thousand White sailors and hundreds of civilian bystanders who attacked innocent African Americans. When the violence ended, five Blacks were dead.

That July, in Washington, DC, rumors of Black men attacking White women riled up White soldiers. "Several hundred soldiers, sailors, and marines participated in the rioting, along with more than a thousand civilians," reported the *New York Times*. "Negroes were hauled from street cars and from automobiles. The Provost Guard was called out, and at 10:20 the police reserves. . . . A number of negroes who were brought bruised and bleeding into police stations were badly frightened and refused to go home except under police escort."

Like virtually all the rest of the White press, the *Atlanta Constitution* assumed that Blacks had been at fault. "Race hatred in the national capital, engineered by attacks on white women by negroes and fanned by three successive nights of rioting, found expression again tonight in clashes between whites and blacks," it reported.

The Black press told a radically different story. As the *Philadelphia Tribune* reported the Washington rampage, "Gangs of sailors, soldiers and civilians ran up and down Pennsylvania Avenue, stomping and beating every colored man they saw." The Baltimore *Afro-American* attributed the trouble to "mobs of white soldiers, sailors and marines, holding the whole colored population of Washington" responsible for the alleged assaults on White women, adding "On Monday, the colored people infuriated by the inability of the police to afford protection retaliated by shooting and beating every white person that came into the Southwest section."

The next week, Chicago exploded after a young Black man wandered into the White section of the beach. The youth was killed. Blacks at a nearby beach went to the White section to confront his suspected murderers, and the city erupted in a race war.

That Tuesday, two days into the violence, the *Chicago Tribune* reported that twenty-seven were known to be dead and hundreds injured: "The first pitched battle of the night occurred at Thirty-fifth and State streets. . . . A small automobile, filled with whites, each armed with a pistol and all firing indiscriminately at blacks, crashed into a patrol wagon at the street intersection." Two of the Whites died as a result, and several policemen were injured.

The *Tribune* noted that "Hundreds of negroes, many carrying personal possessions and some without baggage, joined in an exodus today. The majority of them . . . bought railroad tickets for Memphis and Nashville. A considerable number said they were going to Indianapolis, where, they said, negroes were never disturbed."

At the end of August, the murder of a White woman, supposedly by a Black man who had invaded her home, ignited a riot in Knoxville. A mob marched on the county jail where the suspect was being held with the intention of lynching him. They discovered that authorities had spirited the man away. Guns were drawn, shots were fired, and several people ended up wounded.

The mob then headed to the so-called Negro district, where it attacked pedestrians, broke into shops, and killed two people. National guardsmen called out in response ended up leveling their guns at a group of Blacks fighting with Whites. "Four negroes fell under the machine gunfire," reported the *Atlanta Constitution*.

The madness hit Omaha, Nebraska, in September. There, a Black man, Will Brown, was accused of raping a nineteen-year-old White woman. He was arrested the following day.

Two days later, on Sunday, a mob estimated at several thousand gathered outside the courthouse, which also housed the jail. They demanded that Brown be handed over to them.

The police chief tried to defuse the anger, but the crowd refused to listen. The mayor also tried reasoning with them. The mob attempted to lynch him by hanging him. He was rescued by quick-thinking detectives who cut the rope, leaving him barely alive.

The angry Whites set fire to the building where Brown was being held and refused to let firemen intervene. After nine hours of pandemonium, the police, fearing for their lives and the lives of other prisoners, released Brown to the mob, which promptly hanged him from a telephone poll.

A few days following the insanity in Omaha, commotion erupted in the small town of Elaine, Arkansas. The cause was an attempt by poor Black sharecroppers to unionize in order to get a better price for their cotton. The violence began on September 30 with an organizing meeting at a local Black church. White men showed up, apparently to monitor the meeting. Shooting broke out.

On October 1, Americans awakened to the news that five hundred soldiers from Camp Pike were headed to Elaine to put down a "negro uprising." A series of skirmishes broke out between troops and Black residents, as well as between White vigilantes and Blacks.

The *Atlanta Constitution* described the chaos as "not a racial riot, but insurrection." Local White officials claimed that the "organized negro uprising" had been fostered by a Black man who had preyed "on the ignorance and superstition of a race of children, for monetary gains." The official charged with investigating the affair blamed the "insurrection" on a union group "established for the purpose of banding negroes together for the killing of white people."

By the time Arkansas calmed down, some 150 Blacks were in custody and untold numbers were dead. Eventually the White deaths were put at five, whereas some researchers placed the number of Black victims at more than a hundred. The *Encyclopedia of Arkansas* subsequently labeled the episode "by far the deadliest racial confrontation in Arkansas history and possibly the bloodiest racial conflict in the history of the United States."

Ida Bell Wells-Barnett, a respected Black journalist (also known as Ida B. Wells), produced a version of events totally different from that of the White press. After an exhaustive investigation, she concluded that the whole thing had started with a "peaceful law-abiding hard-working group in their own church, attending strictly to their own business." Without warning, shots had been fired into the church, causing those who were "not killed or wounded" to flee in panic. In the melee, a White man had been shot and killed. The church had been burned down the next day. Wells-Barnett dismissed the story of a Black uprising as absurd: "Had this been a conspiracy of Negroes to kill whites, they would not have started . . . by killing their own members."

In an article in *Current Opinion*, NAACP spokesman Herbert

Seligmann argued that World War 1 had brought rising Black prosperity along with a new determination among Blacks "to achieve their constitutional rights, which had intensified race hatred throughout the South." Given that, he expected severe clashes to continue, but eventually, he wrote, "it will be necessary to recognize his status as a citizen upon which the Negro is going to insist."

———

That August, the *Nation* magazine imagined what a more responsive President Wilson might write in response to the racial violence: He responds with compassion and understanding. He acknowledges that the riots could cast doubt on the United States' sincerity at the "very moment when the covenant of the League of Nations, which will constitute, protect, and advance the new order of the world is being debated." And he criticizes the "failure of the civil authorities to act promptly and to prevent loss of life." He admits that "in each case the white race was the aggressor," which was "the more censurable because our Negro troops are but just back from no little share in carrying our cause and our flag to victory." He expresses regret for "having neglected this vital subject." And he acknowledges that "We cannot undertake the Americanization of those who come to us from abroad if we cannot Americanize ourselves." Finally, he commits to calling together "at once . . . the wisest of both races, that we may counsel together to find the way out and upward."

If there were ever a moment for an American reset on race, it should have been in the aftermath of that calamitous season of racial madness and disharmony after World War I.

Finally, the nation had risen to the status of a superpower and was proudly proclaiming its capacity for moral leadership and its fealty to fairness and humanity. But it was also insisting on the right to torment—rather than extend equality and acceptance to—its most vulnerable citizens. It was asking the world to trust it to be fair to all, even as it was proving itself unworthy of such trust.

For all his pious proclamations, Wilson was a racially unenlightened son of the South who fully believed in Black inferiority. As the historian Kathleen Wolgemuth pointed out in the *Journal of Negro History*:

> When Woodrow Wilson assumed the presidency in 1913 many Negroes believed he would champion their cause for advancement. An unprecedented number of Negroes had cast their vote for Wilson, risking ostracism or ridicule from others of their race for so departing the ranks of the Republican party. . . . Yet it was in Woodrow Wilson's administration that the most bitter blow to Negro hopes of advancement fell: the introduction of segregation into several of the federal departments.

It was accomplished largely covertly: "No executive orders were issued, and changes were discreet and gradual." But the "trickle of news regarding federal segregation soon became a flood. It was becoming apparent . . . that the government's segregation policy was no accident, nor confined to a few separate offices."

The historian Kenneth O'Reilly made the point bluntly: "Nothing could be more debilitating to Wilson's own democratic vision for the nation and the world than the sight of workers tacking up 'White Only' or 'Colored' signs over District of Columbia toilets. Yet that is what Wilson and his people set out to do from the administration's first days."

Wilson and the United States missed a chance—not just to model the ideals that the president so earnestly preached during the final days of war but to save the nation from the rot of racism that had been eating at its core ever since its founders' decision to embrace chattel slavery.

6

WHO DESERVES TO BE AMERICAN?

From the beginning, Americans were unsettled by the idea of a multi-racial citizenry. Despite evidence that the Statute of Liberty (conceived by the abolitionist Édouard René de Laboulaye) may originally have been meant as a tribute to the freedom of formerly enslaved Blacks, the United States saw itself as a fundamentally White nation.

That nervousness about racial integration—and more specifically about granting full membership to non-Whites—never quite went away.

The country's first naturalization act, passed during the second session of the first Congress in March 1790, limited naturalization to "free white" persons who had been in the country at least two years.

Following the Civil War and the granting of citizenship to Blacks by the Fourteenth Amendment, Congress passed the 1870 Naturalization Act, which allowed Blacks to become naturalized citizens but still barred other non-Whites from naturalization. Soon thereafter, most Asians were barred from entering the country.

That process began in 1875 with the passage of the Page Act, named for Horace F. Page, a California congressman out to combat the danger of "cheap Chinese labor and immoral Chinese women." The law imposed a maximum fine of $2,000 and a possible one-year jail sentence for transporting laborers from "China, Japan, or any oriental country, without their free and voluntary consent, for the purpose of holding them to a term of service." It specifically prohibited the immigration of Chinese prostitutes, but it effectively prevented Chinese women, whatever their source of income, from entering the country—which was essentially its purpose.

The *San Francisco Chronicle* traced the origins of the so-called Chinese problem to California's need for labor on the Central Pacific Railroad:

> The Chinese were, in our ignorance of their habits and character, welcomed among us. . . . But a short time passed and we found the tide had become a flood. . . . We found that the incoming crowd of Chinese embraced not only the industrious and decent worker, but then came the gambler, the opium-eater, the prostitute, the criminal and the pauper. In each of our greater cities and lesser valleys there was established a Chinese quarter of filth, prostitution and crime . . . and finally all classes began to see the threatened danger—not only to our trades and industries but to our morals and civilization.

An editorial in the *Nashville Tennessean* was just as blunt: "A landlord will rent a single house in a street to a Chinaman, who at once crowds it to repletion. . . . The atmosphere becomes fetid, and a sickly smell pervades the neighborhood, which causes the tenants of the houses to the right and left to vacate."

Such rhetoric, all too common in the 1870s, eased the way to ever-expanding prohibitions on Chinese immigration. It was virtually indistinguishable from the language that would be used, a generation later, to justify the internment of Japanese Americans during World War II.

———

In 1882, Congress passed the Chinese Exclusion Act, the first of a series of measures aimed at reducing the influx of Chinese that had begun with the California Gold Rush. The act, signed by President Chester A. Arthur on May 6, 1882, prohibited Chinese immigration for ten years—despite critics' complaints that the law violated treaty agreements with China.

The passage of the 1882 measure was accompanied by the same racist rhetoric that had motivated previous anti-Asian measures, although occasionally sane voices rose above the din. *Scientific American* vigorously objected to what it called "anti-Mongolian mania. . . . The picture which Congressmen draw of the certain submergence of Christian civilization in this country by swarming hordes of heathen Chinese is . . . appalling."

Japanese immigration was restricted with the "gentlemen's agreement" of 1907, whereby Japan (under pressure from the US government) agreed to voluntarily suspend most immigration of its nationals to the United States.

Over the decades, Japanese, Syrians, Turks, Asian Indians, and others went to court to make the case that whatever their color or ethnicity appeared to be, they were essentially White.

Reporting on one such case in 1909, the *New York Times* asked, "Is the Turk a White Man?" It explained, "American courts have barred from citizenship Chinese, Japanese, Burmese, and their half breed. Will they bar Turks? . . . The original Turks were of the yellow or

Mongolian race. . . . But in their westward progress the Turks freely intermingled with the Caucasian races whom they subjugated."

As the historian Sarah Gualtieri pointed out in the *Journal of American Ethnic History*, the race of Turkish subjects who were Syrian had not previously been at issue. They had been assumed to be White: "Syrians who had applied for citizenship before 1909 had been granted it without much deliberation. The new decade, however, was different. Anxieties over America's 'foreign element' intensified."

Richard K. Campbell, the commissioner of the US Bureau of Naturalization, ruled that "Syrians and their racial kindred, who are Turkish subjects, were yellow, not white, and that they were barred therefore from naturalization," reported the *Washington Post*. That ruling provoked a statement of protest from the Ottoman chargé d'affaires explaining that experts at the Smithsonian considered "Arabs, Semites, and dwellers of northern Africa" White despite "the fact that the hot sun in that climate has tanned their skins." The State Department agreed with the Smithsonian's experts.

In December 1909, US District Court judge William T. Newman in Atlanta ruled that Costa George Najour was indeed a White man, writing:

> He is not particularly dark, and has none of the characteristics of appearance of the Mongolian race, but, so far as I can see and judge, has the appearance and characteristics of the Caucasian race. . . .
>
> The Assistant United States Attorney, representing the government, objecting to the naturalization of Najour, seems to attach some importance to the fact that the applicant was born within the dominions of Turkey, and was heretofore a subject of the Sultan of Turkey. I do not think this should cut any figure in the matter. If it did, the extension of the Turkish Empire over

people unquestionably of the white race would deprive them of the privilege of naturalization.

The flurry of cases by people of diverse backgrounds from around the world attempting to prove their whiteness, along with the jump in anxiety about the nation's "foreign element," coincided with the rise of eugenics, a suddenly popular pseudoscience that purported to classify and rank people by their ethnicity and racial characteristics.

In February 1917, two months before the United States entered World War I, Congress tweaked the nation's immigration laws to accommodate the rising concerns. The legislation was passed over the veto of Woodrow Wilson, who objected to the literacy test the new law required.

The illiterate were not the only people newly scorned. "Gone is the old, generous sentimental theory, belief, or bit of democratic rhetoric that the United States was 'the asylum of the oppressed,' 'the refuge of the downtrodden,'" observed the *New York Times*. In addition to the literacy test, it opined, the new law included "elaborate and detailed provisions of exclusion, most of which are to be commended": all "'idiots, imbeciles, feeble-minded person, epileptics, insane persons' and so on, paupers, defectives, criminals, the tuberculous, anarchists, these and other exclusions for physical or moral reasons and the welfare of the State will, if faithfully administered, be a national protection."

The new law also excluded many Asians not only already shut out by previous measures by establishing a so-called Asiatic barred zone covering India, Burma, Siam, most of the East Indian and Polynesian islands, and parts of Russia, Arabia, and Afghanistan.

The *Youth's Companion*, a publication aimed at minors, took note of the change in attitude among Americans that had "gradually but surely made immigrants less welcome and unrestricted immigration a menace to our peace and well-being."

Anti-immigrant sentiment only grew once the war ended. The

year 1919 was defined not just by anti-Black riots but by terrorist instigations and anti-immigrant blowback.

In May of that year, bombs in cardboard boxes addressed to various public figures were sent through the mail. The stunt was apparently timed to coincide with the celebration of May Day.

Each bomb "was composed of a wooden cylinder with cover, like those in which medicine bottles may be mailed. Inside were three small sticks of dynamite, several detonating caps of fulminate of mercury, and a small bottle of dark liquid, presumably sulfuric acid," reported the *Independent*, a progressive, weekly magazine then published in New York City.

The bomb sent to the mayor of Seattle did not explode but set off panic and an anxious search for the source. A Black servant, Ethel Williams, opened the box addressed to former Georgia senator Thomas Hardwick and ended up losing both hands. "In addition, she received fearful burns about the face that destroyed one eye and seriously impaired the other," reported the *Atlanta Constitution*. Hardwick's wife suffered severe burns on her face and body.

Sixteen of the bomb boxes, awaiting delivery, were seized in the General Post Office in New York City. Some officials initially thought that the bombs were of German origin, but suspicion ultimately centered on radical groups under the influence of Italian anarchist Luigi Galleani. In all, some thirty-six bombs were discovered.

Bombs again appeared in June. Instead of being sent through the mail, they were deposited right outside the homes of several public officials, including Attorney General A. Mitchell Palmer, who had also been targeted in April. Nine of the explosives went off the evening of June 2.

The bomb planted under the steps of Palmer's Washington home killed a man presumed to be among the bombers. The "remains of the man killed were literally shredded over the block, and driven into the asphalt," reported the *Atlanta Constitution*. Although the explosion caused serious damage to the house, it injured no one inside. The *Atlanta Journal* attributed the violence to "radical agitators" attempting "to inaugurate another reign of terrorism throughout the country."

Palmer had been promoted to attorney general from the relatively obscure position of alien property custodian. He had received a recess appointment after Congress had failed to confirm him. At his swearing-in ceremony at the Supreme Court on March 5, 1919, he had given no clue that he would launch an anti-anarchist crusade.

"The policy of the Department of Justice will be the same as heretofore. It will be a plain, simple attempt by strong Americans working for their country to see that the duty laid upon the Department is properly performed. That duty is to see that the laws are enforced on every man alike, without passion or prejudice, without fear or favor. It will be to enforce laws promptly and expeditiously," he swore before Chief Justice Edward Douglass White.

The bombings, and his own close call, apparently changed Palmer's mind. From late 1919 through early 1920, he presided over a series of raids during which thousands of people—generally immigrants presumed to have radical beliefs—were rounded up and targeted for deportation, most on the basis of no real evidence.

Among Palmer's more dramatic stunts was the mass deportation in December 1919 of 249 alleged anarchists on a ship bound for Russia. The famous anarchist Emma Goldman was among the passengers on the SS *Buford*, which set sail from New York four days before Christmas.

" 'Long live the revolution in America' was chanted defiantly by the motley crowd on the decks of the steel-gray troopship as she churned her way past the Statue of Liberty," reported the *Boston Globe*.

In addition to Palmer, the *New York Times* credited Assistant Attorney General Francis Garvan and William Flynn, the director of the Bureau of Investigation, for the launching of what came to be called the Soviet Ark. Garvan "took office determined to stamp out the Red menace," it reported.

In an article published in *Forum* magazine in February 1920, Palmer made his "Case Against the 'Reds.' " The Communist movement in the United States, he argued, was made up of thousands of aliens who were "direct allies of Trotzky." They were of "misshapen caste of mind and indecencies of character" and dedicated to lawlessness and "criminal autocracy."

Palmer hoped that "American citizens will, themselves, become voluntary agents for us, in a vast organization for mutual defense against the sinister agitation of men and women aliens, who appear to be either in the pay or under the criminal spell of Trotzky and Lenine [Lenin]." He was determined, he wrote, "to drive from our midst the agents of Bolshevism with increasing vigor and with greater speed, until there are no more of them left among us."

Palmer had plenty of company in his hostility to immigrants who were likely to harbor radical thoughts. Indeed, for a while his crusade against Reds and Bolsheviks made him a leading candidate for the 1920 presidential contest. As his unethical tactics came under increasing criticism, enthusiasm for his candidacy faded; but the issue of immigration and the suspicion of immigrants remain a defining characteristic of the era.

The 1920 Republican Party platform favored immigrants "whose standards are similar to ours" and specifically recommended a "higher physical standard" and "more complete exclusion of mental defectives and criminals." The "existing policy of the United States for the exclusion of Asiatic immigrants is sound and should be maintained," declared the platform, which also slammed foreign agitators: "Aliens within the jurisdiction of the United States are not entitled to the right or liberty of agitation against the government or American institutions."

The Democratic Party platform was silent on immigration other than to applaud the US practice of discriminating against Asians as "a true expression of the judgment of our people." The American Federation of Labor praised the Democratic Party platform generally—particularly its support of human rights, working people, and the right to collective bargaining—but complained of its failure to recommend immigration restrictions.

Meanwhile, California politicians lobbied for stronger prohibitions against Japanese immigration. At congressional hearings in the summer of 1920, California senator James Phelan equated the Japanese with other acknowledged undesirables: "If urging their exclusion from California is regarded as persecution, then the same would apply to the Chinese; it would apply to the reds and the anarchists and the unfit of all races and classes. It is not persecution; it is preservation."

California governor William D. Stephens complained that the "fecundity of the Japanese race far exceeds that of any other people that we have in our midst." And California's leading newspapers pummeled the Japanese with disparaging headlines: "Imperial Valley Is Aroused over the Japanese Menace"; "Japanese Plan Invasion of Industrial Fields."

That July, the arrival of some forty Japanese "picture brides" in San Francisco became fodder for a *Los Angeles Times* article on the "Oriental Menace" that voiced a local attorney's peculiarly specific fear that Japanese immigration would lead to "joy rides of big Japanese boys and American girls."

In a statement issued in December 1920 and published in full in the *New York Tribune,* Commissioner of Immigration Frederick A. Wallis suggested that an amendment to the Constitution might be needed to keep European rabble out. "More than ten million are now waiting in various parts of war stricken Europe to swarm to the United States as soon as they can obtain transportation. . . . I am inclined to believe there are more like fifteen million . . . clamoring to come to America. Many thousands of them already have bought steamship tickets," he claimed, adding that it was essential to weed out undesirables: "I would rather send back a thousand good men than let one bad man come into the country. Our slogan is, 'When in doubt, deport.' "

Wallis also criticized the US literacy test as a "farce." It had done nothing to weed out immigrant riffraff, he said. "Most of the . . . anarchists that we had penned up here a few days ago could read and write. . . . There is no safety to the country in such tests. We need something more practical."

The *Literary Digest* echoed Wallis's concern, fretting over the loss of the "American type" if the nation had to absorb millions of European refugees.

Spurred on by relentless anti-immigrant propaganda, the House of Representatives considered various measures to restrict immigration for time periods ranging from six months to two years. In early December, the House Committee on Immigration and Nationalization approved a bill setting a two-year freeze on immigration. That December, the full House passed a measure that would have imposed a one-year immigration ban.

The Senate leaned toward a different approach, one that limited immigration by ethnicity and would favor northern and western European countries such as England, Ireland, and Germany over places like Italy, Poland, and Russia. The Senate passed its own bill allocating immigration slots by ethnic percentages. After rapid approval by the House, the measure was sent to the ailing President Wilson, who failed to sign it.

In May 1921, Congress passed an essentially equivalent bill, which Wilson's successor, Warren G. Harding, signed within days of its passage. The bill limited immigration from each country to 3 percent of each country's immigrants present in the United States in 1910. The quota did not apply to tourists, diplomats, minor children of citizens, aliens from Asian countries excluded by prior legislation, or those whose numbers were regulated by treaty (such as the Japanese). Nor did it cover the Americas. Congress had no desire to create friction with its northern neighbor by suddenly changing the rules, and no one expected huge numbers to come from Mexico, the Caribbean, or Central and South America.

A few critics thought the legislation, driven by immigration hysteria, was designed to address a problem that did not exist. The *Forum* magazine pointed out that, despite all the anti-immigrant rhetoric circulating, no one had presented convincing evidence that immigration was out of control. The *New York Times*, among many other publications, praised the new policy:

> On the surface there is nothing "scientific" in the basic provision of the new law that in any year the number of immigrants shall not exceed 3 percent of the number of their nationals already in the United States; but in reality the provision will result in a selection generally conforming to the best judgment of authorities on the subject. The great menace of the new immigration of recent years is that, by introducing large numbers of various races whose languages and traditions are alien, the nation may lose unity and solidarity. . . . Tens of thousands from the East and South of Europe will be barred. Of immigrants from the West and North of Europe there will doubtless be admitted as many as apply and can pass the tests of personal fitness.

The 1921 law became the template for the 1924 revision, which, after Congress took a hard look at the issue of ethnic desirability, locked the quota policy into place. That hard look meant plunging into the fetid swamp of racial superiority research.

That research, dating back to the late 1800s, was essentially an effort to justify bigotry scientifically. The United States' most prominent eugenics researchers were thoroughly convinced that northern and western Europeans had the best blood lines, and that all other "races" were inferior. They feared pollution by those inferior races and the decline of the United States as a consequence. Congress turned to those so-called experts for advice as it crafted the 1924 law.

Lothrop Stoddard, a Ku Klux Klan member with a PhD in history from Harvard and author of *The Rising Tide of Color Against White World-Supremacy*, was among the most distinguished of that group. Madison Grant, who had earned an undergraduate degree at Yale and a law degree from Columbia, was another highly respected expert. In *The Passing of the Great Race; Or, the Racial Basis of European History*, published in 1916, Grant argued that inferior races were displacing the "Nordic" race in the United States to the severe detriment and perhaps ultimate demise of the country:

> During the last century the New England manufacturer imported the Irish and French Canadian and the resultant fall in the New England birthrate at once became ominous. The refusal of the native American to work with his hands when he can hire or import serfs to do manual labor for him is the prelude to his extinction and the immigrant laborers are now breeding out their masters and killing by filth and by crowding as effectively as by the sword.

In his introduction to Lothrop's *The Rising Tide of Color Against White World-Supremacy*, published in 1920, Grant further advanced that argument:

> The great hope of the future here in America lies in the realization of the working class that competition of the Nordic with the alien is fatal, whether the latter be the lowly immigrant from southern or eastern Europe or whether he be the more obviously dangerous Oriental against whose standards of living

the white man cannot compete. . . . Democratic ideals among an homogeneous population of Nordic blood, as in England or America, is one thing, but it is quite another for the white man to share his blood with, or entrust his ideals to, brown, yellow, black, or red men. This is suicide pure and simple.

In the main text, Stoddard built on that theory, claiming that World War I had unified the inferior races in solidarity "against the dominant white man. . . . The colored world suddenly saw the white peoples which, in racial matters, had hitherto maintained something of a united front, locked in an internecine death-grapple of unparalleled ferocity . . . it saw white race-unity cleft by political and moral gulfs."

Stoddard quoted an *Atlantic* article by the Black sociologist W.E.B. Du Bois, who wrote, "The War of the Color Line will outdo in savage inhumanity any war this world has yet seen," turning Du Bois's condemnation of the plundering of Africa and his appeal for peace and justice into what sounds like a prophecy of race war.

In his testimony before Congress, Stoddard continued his alarmist rhetoric, calling for "still more restrictive legislation . . . to stay the flood."

When asked about the assimilability of the foreign horde, he specifically excluded England and France before replying "All of these people are in a very unassimilable state of mind."

In his testimony, Madison Grant made similar points: "There is no good reason why the Latin-American countries to the south of us, which in some cases furnish very undesirable immigrants, should have preferential treatment over, let us say, Scandinavia or England. The Mexicans who come into the United States are overwhelmingly of Indian blood, and the recent intelligence tests have shown their very low intellectual status. We have already got too many of them in the Southwestern States."

Thomas Phillips, a congressman from Pennsylvania, observed,

"Our civilization can be sustained and our ideals can be perpetuated only by maintaining or creating conditions that preserve the race that created these ideals and built up that civilization."

With the help of such testimony, Congress convinced itself that racial/ethnic quotas were essential. The bill passed both Houses of Congress on May 15 with veto-proof majorities, 308 to 58 in the House and 69 to 9 in the Senate.

With the Immigration Act of 1924, the United States formally adopted a scheme designed to keep the nation as White as possible, even as it reduced the numbers of low-quality Europeans. The new quota would be based on 2 percent of the number of foreign-born individuals by nationality living in the United States in 1890. After July 1927, the basis of the "national origins" quota was to become the 1920 census, with national origin to be determined by country of "birth or ancestry."

The calculation specifically excluded residents who were "descendants of slave immigrants or the descendants of American aborigines" as well as "aliens ineligible to citizenship or their descendants." It also excluded immigrants from areas specifically specified as undesirable. The quotas effectively "excised all nonwhite, non-European people . . . erasing them from the American nationality," observed the historian Mae M. Ngai.

President Calvin Coolidge, who had taken office in 1923, strongly objected to the provisions excluding Japanese, a situation he preferred to handle through diplomatic negotiations. But he nonetheless signed the bill. In doing so, he gave his blessing to a scheme that would become the center of US immigration policy for two generations.

The face the United States was presenting to the world was one of unremitting intolerance and bigotry, doubling down on what was comfortable and familiar. And it was doing so in the name of American greatness.

7

A NEW DEAL FOR WHOM?

As the 1920s roared to a close, America was ablaze with hope. "No Congress of the United States . . . has met with a more pleasing prospect than that which appears at the present time," declared President Calvin Coolidge in his State of the Union address in December 1928. ". . . The country can . . . anticipate the future with optimism."

Herbert Hoover, Coolidge's successor, was equally bullish. "Through liberation from widespread poverty we have reached a higher degree of individual freedom than ever before," he said during his inauguration address in 1929. The challenge ahead was to "establish more firmly stability and security of business and employment and thereby remove poverty."

Six months after Hoover took office, the stock market imploded. "Stock prices virtually collapsed yesterday, swept downward with gigantic losses in the most disastrous trading day in the stock market's history," reported the *New York Times*. Hoover called on Americans to stick it out. The crisis became a catastrophe.

In December 1931, facing pressure from a panicked nation, Hoover asked Congress to create a new agency, the Reconstruction Finance Corporation. With an initial budget of $500 million and authority to borrow up to $2 billion, the RFC would be charged with granting loans to railroads, banks, mortgage associations, and other institutions to re-invigorate banks, enable farmers to postpone mortgage payments, and stimulate the economy. Hoover signed the bill in January, promising that it would "stop deflation in agriculture and industry and thus . . . increase employment by the restoration of men to their normal jobs."

The next month, in a radio address celebrating Abraham Lincoln's birthday, Hoover acknowledged that the United States was suffering through one of the most challenging periods since Lincoln's time: "We are engaged in a fight upon a hundred fronts." But he was "confident of the resources, the power, and the courage of our people to triumph."

Hoover easily won renomination that June at the Republican National Convention in Chicago. The crowd, twelve thousand strong, chanted his name for twenty-seven minutes. In the telegram accepting his nomination, he pledged to confront "the effects of the worldwide storm which has devastated us with trials and suffering unequalled in but few periods of our history."

Less than two weeks later, the Democrats convened, also in Chicago. The party's nominee, Franklin D. Roosevelt, broke precedent by showing up personally. His acceptance speech indicted Republicans' incompetence. He promised "a new deal for the American people."

During the campaign, Roosevelt charged the Hoover administration with having caused the Depression and accused Hoover of waging a "campaign of fear."

Hoover lashed out at Roosevelt's "fantastic, frivolous promises" of federal jobs for the 10 million unemployed. "It is a promise no government could fulfill," said Hoover, who accused Roosevelt of presenting "oratory, instead of the facts."

———

Although African Americans had traditionally favored Republicans, many were intrigued by the possibilities of a Roosevelt presidency.

The Great Depression was hitting Blacks especially hard. In the North, unskilled Black workers faced increased competition from Whites, whose skin color gave them an advantage with White employers. And Blacks in the South—where the majority of them lived—generally owned no land. Only a fifth were landowners. The rest were disproportionately tenant farmers and sharecroppers.

Blacks were not only concerned about deliverance from the misery of the Great Depression but wanted unimpeded access to the voting booth, an end to discrimination in its various forms, and protection from racist lynch mobs. None of that was in the Republican agenda.

Prior to the Democratic and Republican conventions, the NAACP had tried to get both parties to commit to a "Negro plank" in their respective platforms. The Black political class was increasingly annoyed with the Republican Party's taking Blacks for granted.

Roger Didier of the *Pittsburgh Courier* evoked the frustration in a column on the Republican National Convention: "What did the party pledge about lynching? Nothing. What did the party pledge about disfranchisement? Nothing. What did the party pledge about education? Nothing. What did the party pledge about fairness in the civil service? Nothing. What did the party pledge about discrimination in any or all forms? Nothing."

The so-called Negro plank in the Republican Party platform simply said that the party was a longtime "friend of the American Negro" and pledged to "maintain equal opportunity and rights for our Negro citizens."

But for all the Republican Party's faults, the Democratic Party wasn't much of an alternative. The Democratic National Convention featured no Black speakers, and its platform did not address race—despite passionate pleas to the resolutions committee from the tiny cadre of Blacks who attended.

The Democratic Party's reluctance to engage on racial issues stemmed from an unavoidable fact: southern segregationists considered the party their own. Any plan to mobilize Black voters inevitably encountered resistance from the South—where the vast majority of Blacks lived but where very few were allowed to vote.

As the *Afro-American* put it, "It is easily possible for a . . . majority of the voters of the nation to be overridden by a decided minority . . . [because] of the disfranchisement of blacks. . . . One white man in South Carolina outvotes six or seven white men in Connecticut—because the South Carolina white man votes not only for himself but also for disfranchised black men."

Still, there was intense speculation leading up to the 1932 election that Blacks might finally leave the Republican Party and throw their support to Roosevelt—especially in light of what was beginning to be seen, in some quarters, as a possible Roosevelt rout.

The highly respected *Literary Digest* reader poll had Roosevelt ahead in forty-one states and winning 474 Electoral College votes to Hoover's 57.

Hoover's criticisms of Roosevelt remained unrelenting to the end. "Those men and women who have supported the party over these many years should not be led astray by false gods arrayed in the rainbow colors of promises," he told the nation by radio from Elko, Nevada, on November 7.

Nonetheless, as the *Literary Digest* had projected, the candidate of rainbow-colored promises won in a landslide. Roosevelt got 22.8 million votes to Hoover's 15.8 million, winning the Electoral College 472 to 59. Democrats also captured the Senate and expanded their majority in the House. The *Washington Post* termed the victory "the most sweeping landslide in history."

In the end, even as Whites overwhelmingly voted for Roosevelt, Blacks were loyal to the party of Lincoln. A postelection analysis by the *Atlanta Daily World* estimated that Roosevelt and other Democrats had garnered only a third of the Black vote. The report was based on a tabulation of returns "from the metropolitan centers of those states where Negroes are protected in their right of franchise."

But even though Hoover won the lion's share of Black votes, he received significantly fewer than Republican candidates generally received. As the *World* noted, "New York, Philadelphia, Pittsburgh, Cleveland, Detroit, St. Louis, Chicago and Los Angeles all reported stunning gains" for Democrats. The *World* saw the shift away from Republicans as evidence of Blacks deciding "that more than one basket is necessary to carry their eggs to market."

———

Two days after the election, Roosevelt announced a period of self-imposed passivity. He promised to wait at least two months before selecting a cabinet. "Until January 1, 1933, the greater part of my time will be occupied with my duties as Governor of the State of New York."

On inauguration day, March 4, a cool and cloudy Saturday, Roosevelt declared, "This great Nation will endure as it has endured, will revive and will prosper. So first of all let me assert my firm belief that the only thing we have to fear is fear itself,—nameless, unreasoning, unjustified terror which paralyzes needed efforts to convert retreat into advance."

He pledged to send Congress "measures that a stricken Nation in the midst of a stricken world may require" and to urge their speedy adoption. Should Congress fail, he would request "broad Executive power to wage a war against the emergency, as great as the power that would be given to me if we were in fact invaded by a foreign foe."

In the days leading up to the inauguration, some forty states had declared banking holidays in order to stop a rash of withdrawals. Roosevelt said that he would extend the closings long enough to put emergency measures into place.

Congress reconvened the Thursday following his inauguration. Roosevelt got straight to the point. He asked for the "immediate enactment" of legislation giving him control over banks. By the *New York Times*' reckoning, it took only eight hours and thirty-seven minutes for both houses of Congress to pass (and for the president to sign) the Emergency Banking Act. The new law gave the president the power to forbid the hoarding of gold, to issue new money, and to exercise tighter control over national banks. It also paved the way for creation of federal deposit insurance.

"One week from the day when Franklin D. Roosevelt assumed the office of President of the United States, he will have been invested by . . . Congress as a Constitutional dictator," concluded *New York Times* Washington correspondent Arthur Krock.

In a page-one summation of the event, the *Times* declared, "It was a grim Congress which met today, the most momentous gathering of the country's legislators since war was declared in 1917. . . . [They] hurled against the enemy of depression and despondency a weapon which they hoped would penetrate the subtle armor of an allegorical or Bunyanlike antagonist.

"Congress hardly knew what it passed today," added the *Times*. The House had no copies of the measure so, it "was read and explained on the floor by Representative [Henry Bascom] Steagall." The legislators, opined the *Times*, "were glad to place the responsibility for action in the hands of one man." That man—Roosevelt—was happy to seize the moment, even if he was working without a playbook and banking largely on impulse and hope.

In his first fireside chat, the Sunday after the banking legislation passed, Roosevelt assured his radio audience that it was "safer to keep your money in a reopened bank than under the mattress." On March 20, a week and a day later, he signed the Economy Act, which approved cuts of just over $500 million in the salaries of federal employees and benefits to nondisabled war veterans. No official signing ceremony was held. Roosevelt received the bill while lunching at his desk with Federal Farm Board chairman Henry Morgenthau, Jr. Turning from his bowl of soup, Roosevelt managed to sign the legislation "after several ineffectual scratchings with a common pen. . . . He told his secretary, Stephen T. Early, that the pen must be 'one of those old post office stubs.' Smiling, the President said: 'That is a good job done,' " reported the *Times*.

Over the next several months, Roosevelt pushed a staggering array of measures through Congress, creating a flurry of political and legislative action unlike anything Americans had ever seen.

Two days after signing the Economy Act, Roosevelt signed the Beer and Wine Revenue Act, aimed at raising some $150 million in tax revenue by legalizing low-alcohol beer and wine, which the Eighteenth Amendment had made illegal. "I hope you got the smile at the end," Roosevelt quipped to press photographers as he signed the measure. Later that year, the states ratified the Twenty-first Amendment, which repealed Prohibition altogether.

On March 14, Roosevelt told his chief speechwriter, Raymond Moley, of a brainstorm he'd had "only the night before . . . to put platoons of young unemployed men to work in the forests and national parks," according to Michael Hiltzik author of *The New Deal: A Modern History*. A week after that conversation, he formally proposed the Emergency Conservation Work Act, which mandated the creation of the Civilian Conservation Corps. Congress passed it by voice vote ten days later after accepting an amendment from Representative Oscar Stanton De Priest, America's sole Black congressman, prohibiting discrimination based on "race, creed or color." Roosevelt signed the measure immediately. "This law will not only relieve unemployment but will also promote a much-needed activity in this country," he said.

The plan was to sign up unmarried young men and send them into America's national forests. They would restore the parks and put a little money into their pockets while bolstering their work ethic.

The Agricultural Adjustment Act, submitted to Congress on March 16 and signed on May 12, strove to stabilize the prices of farm products. It enabled the government to buy livestock and crops, or pay farmers to destroy them, in order to keep prices up. The legislation would provide loans to farmers through the Federal land banks, with money drawn from a special $200 million fund for the benefit of farmers who were facing, or had experienced, foreclosure. It also gave the government authority to issue up to $3 billion in new currency and to "reduce the gold content of the dollar by as much as 50 percent"—which was a huge step in moving the United States away from the gold standard. The *New York Times* observed that the legislation gave Roosevelt "the widest range of authority over the economic affairs of the nation ever granted to a President in peace time."

As a result of the new initiatives, a starving nation witnessed the somewhat unsettling sight of farmers plowing under thousands of acres of cotton and delivering young pigs for early slaughter.

May also saw the creation of the Tennessee Valley Authority. It was a triumph built on the carcass of a fiasco. Roosevelt signed the TVA Act (also known as the Muscle Shoals Bill) on May 18, even as the Justice Department was investigating the private utilities that had been leasing the Muscle Shoals water plant and were suspected of having damaged it through misuse.

The legislation gave the Tennessee Valley Authority unheard-of power, enabling it to "acquire real estate for the construction of dams, reservoirs, transmission lines, power houses, and other structures, and navigation projects," manufacture explosives, and much more. The dream was to take a poor, suffering region of the country and make it into a model of possibility and progress.

"Like the ancient king who dipped seven times in the Jordan . . . , the Senate dipped seven times in the Tennessee River . . . creating a Tennessee Valley Authority [that] goes far beyond the original Muscle Shoals project," commented the *Philadelphia Inquirer*.

The final major legislation of Roosevelt's first season of labors was the Industrial Recovery Act. The president signed it on June 16.

In presenting the bill to the Senate Finance Committee in May, New York senator Robert Wagner had explained that it would spur industry to improve wages and working conditions and otherwise foster a better workplace, motivated in part by "direct Government expenditures for public works."

The measure, as amended, was stronger than Wagner's proposal. It gave the president a huge amount of power over private industry, including the power to set standards with "codes of fair competition," to set the length of the workday, to impose consumer protections, to set limits on imports, and to establish minimum wages in trades or industries that seemed out of line. It even allowed him, indirectly, to "control the operations of oil pipelines."

The bill also created a Federal Emergency Administration of Public Works (which later became the Public Works Administration) to employ people through public works programs fixing highways, constructing public buildings, preserving soil, developing waterpower, building low-cost housing, and doing an array of other things.

Before the National Industrial Recovery Act passed, the *Wall Street Journal* had worried about the "broad powers that would be granted the President." After Roosevelt signed it, the *Los Angeles Times* dryly observed that "the powers granted to the President are essentially those of an economic dictator."

In signing the legislation, Roosevelt set a goal of measurably decreasing employment "before winter comes." He called the legislation "the most important attempt of this kind in history" and declared that it would present the nation with a "simple but vital test:—'Must we go on in many groping, disorganized, separate units to defeat or shall we move as one great team to victory?' "

In a period of less than four months, Roosevelt had not only renegotiated the relationship of two supposedly equal branches of government, he had redefined the very role of government—extending its reach into corners of people's lives where it previously had been deemed neither needed nor desired. A nation filled with millions of people who were hungry, broke, and devoid of clear prospects had not just accepted this new notion of government but eagerly embraced it, along with the idea of a social safety net—even though no one at the time called it that.

———

Roosevelt had never promised that in taking on the Great Depression he would also tackle American inequality. But it quickly became clear that unless he did, the New Deal might actually make things worse—simply because discrimination was so tightly woven into the fabric of American society. Almost immediately the National Recovery Administration became embroiled in controversy over allegations that its policies were leading to the firing of Blacks and the hiring of Whites for jobs that—thanks to the president's policies—suddenly offered higher wages. A job's pay depended on how it was coded. As Howard University professor Kelly Miller explained in a letter to the *Baltimore Sun*, "In several of these codes . . . lurked sinister discrimination against what is understood to be Negro jobs." In the textile industry, for example, employers aimed to remove "cleaners" from minimum-wage protection, since cleaners were generally Black.

In Memphis, the NAACP complained about businesses firing Blacks because a $14 salary was deemed "more than a Negro should have." In Arkansas, White farmers were "sending their sons to the civil conservation camps where they receive $30 a month, and hiring our people to do the farm work at $10 to $15 a month," reported the *Chicago Defender*. The National Recovery Act, argued Professor Miller, "cannot promote national recovery in this way."

The Agricultural Adjustment Act became mired in a similar controversy. By giving cotton plantation owners an incentive to reduce or eliminate their cotton crop, the act drove Black tenant farmers into poverty. "Many black sharecroppers who should have received reimbursements never received them because these reimbursements were held by the planters as payment for rents, or by store owners as payment for bills, or were never distributed by local officials. What were common discriminatory practices in the South were sanctioned by and institutionalized in national legislation," the sociologist Stephen Valocchi pointed out.

The Tennessee Valley Authority was also criticized for discriminatory practices. TVA employees were supposedly hired on the basis of a merit system, but in at least one area few Blacks took the qualifying exam because word circulated that the exam was for Whites only.

At Norris Dam in Tennessee, the TVA built a permanent community for workers with large, comfortable houses and beautiful views. But Blacks were not allowed to live in those lovely houses since Tennessee's constitution prohibited Black and White children from attending the same schools. Blacks were housed elsewhere in barracks.

The National Housing Act, argued Valocchi, "expanded mortgage loan guarantees for working and middle-class families but . . . did so in a way that fostered segregation and excluded blacks from equal access to the federally insured mortgage market."

Many of the programs, which were thrown together in a haphazard manner, were initiated with no thought given to their unintended consequences. Also, Roosevelt, unwilling to alienate his base of southern White supporters, was loath to take actions that might seem solicitous of Blacks. But as pressure from Black critics mounted, he gingerly began reaching out to Black leadership.

In October 1935, Roosevelt wrote to several Black ministers in Baltimore requesting advice on "how the government can better serve." Several responded by suggesting that he take on lynching and also discrimination in Great Society programs.

In an interview with the *Afro-American*, several of the pastors shared their letters or thoughts. The Reverend Robert Brooks wrote, "Mobs continue to overpower officers of the law and lynch helpless victims on the least provocation." He suggested legislation "making it a federal crime to take life without due process of law."

Brooks also criticized Jim Crow practices in the Civilian Conservation Corps: "Out of more than 300,000 assembled in these camps, not more than 20,000 are colored and these are denied the privilege of having their own racial group in the capacity of officers," he pointed out.

In early 1933, Roosevelt moved affirmatively to address the swirl of racial issues by asking Interior Secretary Harold Ickes, who was responsible for the Public Works Administration, to appoint someone to oversee the treatment of Blacks. Ickes hired Clark Foreman, whose grandfather had founded the *Atlanta Constitution*, as special adviser on the economic status of Negroes. Foreman had earned a PhD in political science from Columbia University with a thesis titled "Environmental Factors in Negro Elementary Education." Foreman selected Robert Weaver, a Black economics professor with a new doctorate from Harvard, as his associate. Weaver became a leader of the Interdepartmental Group Concerned with the Special Problems of the Negro Population. Shortly thereafter, Weaver moved into Foreman's job.

In December 1935, the *Norfolk Journal and Guide* took notice of Weaver. The article, headlined "Interior Dept. Negro Advisor Has Been Busy," cited Ickes's annual report, which credited Weaver with attacking anti-Black discrimination in the Public Works Administration and working with the housing division to ensure Black participation. The *Atlanta Daily World* was also laudatory of Weaver's work on "slum clearance and low cost housing," observing "Negroes are sharing generously in the program which is being pushed in a number of cities in various sections of the country."

Such stories generated goodwill among Blacks not only for Weaver but for the president he served. As the historian Harvard Sitkoff has observed, "However limited and tentative they may seem in retrospect, the New Deal's steps toward racial justice and equality were unprecedented and were judged most favorably by blacks at the time."

Washington Post columnist Charles Lane has accurately noted that the New Deal did not launch a frontal assault on discrimination or undo restrictive racial covenants. Judged by today's standards, the steps Roosevelt took toward racial equality were modest. But Roosevelt and his people brought Blacks to the table in a way no other administration had. And by 1936, Democrats were looking a lot more appealing than Republicans to many African Americans. That year's elections became a racial referendum on the political parties.

The Republican National Convention, which met in Cleveland in early June, was immediately embroiled in controversy over the credentials committee's decision to seat "lily-white" delegations from Florida, Georgia, Louisiana, and North Carolina. A group calling itself the National Anti-Lily White League wrote a letter to the committee objecting to what it called a decision "based on the color of the contestants rather than merits of the case."

The dispute quickly became ugly. Perry Howard, a Black national committeeman from Mississippi, was among those contending to be seated. White Mississippians accused him of irregularities in the handling of federal patronage and of not even living in Mississippi. Howard survived the challenge. A White delegation leader from South Carolina did not. J. C. Hambright, also a national committee member, was attacked with his own words, as revealed in a letter he had written to his brother. As the *Pittsburgh Courier* reported the imbroglio, Hambright's letter, which was read to the credentials committee in executive session, was "packed with insulting references to Negroes and to leaders of the Hoover administration." Hambright's language was so coarse that committee members felt compelled to unseat his delegate group.

"This decision has removed the threat of an outright revolt on the floor of the convention on the 'Lily White' issue," concluded the *New York Herald Tribune*.

As had become its custom, the NAACP submitted platform suggestions to both political parties. The first item on the list was a pledge to pass anti-lynching legislation. The NAACP also asked that the parties condemn discrimination in relief programs and federal employment projects, that Congress enforce the Fourteenth and Fifteenth Amendments, that the civil service use fingerprints instead of photographs for purposes of identification, and that the federal government abolish all discrimination in allocation of funds for education. Neither party came close to making such commitments.

Although the Republican Party platform attacked the New Deal as a violation of the "rights and liberties of American citizens," it had nothing to say about lynching, voter disenfranchisement, or racial discrimination in federal programs. Instead, it endorsed "equal opportunity for our colored citizens," pledged "protection of their economic status and personal safety," and promised to "do our best to further their employment." It also promised to make every effort to "ameliorate living conditions" for "our Indian population."

The Democrats, whose convention convened in Philadelphia, essentially ignored the NAACP request. Instead, its platform condemned Republicans and embraced a "democracy of opportunity for all the people." The Democrats did make one gesture toward racial inclusion. For the first time they seated Black delegates and alternates.

The Democrats presumably assumed that they could afford to be cavalier with the NAACP's request, as they had Roosevelt, the closest thing Americans had seen to a political hero in a long time. Roosevelt had already won the hearts of many African Americans.

The *New York Times*, in August 1936, noted that more Blacks would vote in South Carolina than at any point in the past forty years and that they would likely vote for Roosevelt. A member of the Richmond County Board of Registration told the *Times*, "Every Negro I have registered so far has said he would vote for President Roosevelt. They say Roosevelt saved them from starvation, gave them aid when they were in distress, and now they are going to vote for him."

Alfred Landon, the Republican torchbearer, was a huge question mark—and not just to Blacks. The Kansas governor and former businessman was far from a household name. Immediately after his nomination, Postmaster General James Farley ridiculed Landon as "one of the least known of the Governors of the forty-eight states." In a statement issued by the Democratic National Committee, Farley said the Republican ticket was the weakest "ever nominated in the history of the party. . . . Every single Republican who had had a part in shaping party policies . . . was passed over in favor of a man who eighteen months ago was unheard of."

In a lengthy *Ladies' Home Journal* profile, Milton MacKaye focused on Landon's lack of celebrity luster: "A year ago he was the kindly regarded but obscure governor of a Midwestern state. . . . Today he is a presidential nominee." One reason he had risen to the top, speculated MacKaye, was that voters sought "quiet after the clangor and alarums of the past four years, peace after the battles and skull-splittings, calm after the excitement."

Born in West Middlesex, Pennsylvania, to a father who was an independent oil executive, Landon had moved to Kansas with his family because of oil. He had gone to law school, served time as a banker, and eventually become a successful oilman. His entry into politics had been almost accidental: he had taken a six-week break from business to work as secretary for then governor Henry J. Allen, and the job had sold him on politics. He had run for governor in 1932 in part to unite the divided Kansas Republican Party. Somewhere along the way, he had decided he could do a better job than Roosevelt.

Landon's lack of history with Hoover gave some Republicans hope that he could win the contest with Roosevelt. He secured the nomination with only nineteen votes against him.

John Hamilton, Landon's campaign manager and strategist, gave the nominating speech. Hamilton's "mention of Landon's name started a prairie fire of enthusiasm among the delegates," reported the *New York Times*. Two parades, one lasting twenty-eight minutes, erupted in his honor.

The enthusiasm inside did not reflect the sentiment outside. Landon, an earnest but uninspired speaker, was not anyone's idea of a firebrand or charismatic leader. In complimenting a speech that he gave in Kansas that July, the *Christian Science Monitor* observed, "There is not a shred of bombast in its 3500 words."

At the end of October, in one of the final appearances of the campaign, Landon succeeded in drawing a huge, passionate crowd to New York's Madison Square Garden. Police put the number of people who showed up to greet him at more than 60,000, with perhaps 22,000 making it into the hall.

Landon pledged allegiance to liberty, the Supreme Court, free enterprise, and the Bill of Rights. He took on the New Deal, denouncing its "price fixing," its "choking" of business, its bolstering of "private monopoly," and its practice of "spending more than it takes in."

He called out Roosevelt: "I say to him: Mr. President, I am willing to trust the people. . . . I am against the concentration of power in the hands of the Chief Executive. Tell us where you stand, Mr. President. Tell us not in generalities, but clearly, so that no one can mistake your meaning. And tell us why you have evaded the issue until the eve of the election."

Two days later, Roosevelt appeared in the same venue, which was again filled to capacity. After a thirteen-minute standing ovation (compared to ten minutes for Landon), Roosevelt served up a powerful defense of his record:

> Tonight I call the roll—the roll of honor of those who stood with us in 1932 and still stand with us today.
>
> Written on it are the names of millions who never had a chance . . . those who despaired, young men and young women for whom opportunity had become a will-o'-the-wisp . . . farmers whose acres yielded only bitterness, business men whose books were portents of disaster; home owners who were faced with eviction. . . .
>
> Their hopes have become our record.

The *New York Times* pronounced the president "in his best oratorical form." His voice "carried a fighting tone as he declared his intention of pushing forward his program of reforms, it trembled once or twice as he spoke of the condition of the masses, and it rose to a solemn tone as he delivered his peroration on a note of devotion to the nation."

Three days later, Americans reelected Roosevelt in the most one-sided presidential contest of the modern era. Roosevelt won 28 million votes to Landon's 17 million. He carried every state except New Hampshire and Vermont and won 523 electoral votes to Landon's 8. The Democrats also increased their number to a three-fourths majority in the House and a 69 to 22 majority in the Senate.

No major poll had predicted such a sweeping victory. The previously highly regarded *Literary Digest* pollsters were humiliated. Its final poll results, released only days before the election, had had Landon winning in a landslide: 370 electoral votes to Roosevelt's 161. Wilfred Funk, the *Digest*'s editor in chief, pronounced himself "astounded." Tennessee senator Kenneth McKellar demanded a Senate investigation and called for a "federal supervisory committee" to oversee all such polling in the future.

New York Times writer W. A. Warn wondered whether Roosevelt's overwhelming victory "signed the death warrant of traditional political Democracy in this country and the traditional two-party political set-up dominant in the politics of the nation from the start."

The election obviously did not herald the death of the two-party system, but it destroyed the widespread assumption that Americans were inalterably opposed to big government, that American pluck and self-reliance left no room for a safety net; and it shattered, seemingly forever, the close alignment between the Black community and the Republican Party.

As Nancy J. Weiss pointed out in *Farewell to the Party of Lincoln: Black Politics in the Age of FDR*, Roosevelt "won 81 percent of the black vote in Harlem, 75 percent in black neighborhoods in Pittsburgh, 69 percent in Philadelphia, 66 percent in Detroit, 65 percent in Cincinnati, 60 percent in Cleveland, and 49 percent in Chicago. . . . Roosevelt won anywhere from 60 to 250 percent more votes in black neighborhoods in major cities in 1936 than in 1932."

Earl Brown, writing in the *New York Amsterdam News*, observed, "Not only in the North but also in the South the Negroes went to the polls in greater numbers than ever before. . . . If the Negro's political activity in the South last Tuesday was a harbinger of better times in that section, his efforts in the North were nothing short of revolutionary. He proved at the polls that he, like the majority of American voters, demands liberal government."

The NAACP released a statement suggesting that the vote showed there was no point in catering to the South's White supremacists:

Mr. Roosevelt's victory was so overwhelming that he is the first Democratic President in history who could have been elected had not a single vote been cast for him by the solid South. This circumstance should free Mr. Roosevelt and the enlightened wing of the Democratic party from control of the South of the Cotton Ed Smiths, the Bilbos, and the Talmadges. The abolition of the two-thirds rule by the Democratic convention, which rule has permitted the South hitherto to exercise veto power on many presidential candidates, and the new mobility of the Negro vote . . . can mean a new deal politically for the Negro.

Debate will likely rage forever over how much impact Roosevelt's New Deal had on ending the Depression; but without question, it changed America in fundamental ways: it presented a vision of progressive government that was not only benign but essential, and it told a people who had soured on the utterly unresponsive Republican Party that America, at last, might be willing to consider giving Blacks a fair shake. The vote for Roosevelt was not just a vote for an inspirational individual; it was a vote for faith in an American possibility not yet seen, a prayer that some viable notion of real equality was finally taking root in soil too frequently fertilized by needlessly spilled Black blood.

NAACP executive secretary Walter White pointed out that the margin of Roosevelt's victory freed him of any need to cater to the White South, and he warned that unless something was done about lynching, unemployment, and discrimination in virtually all sectors of government, the Black vote was likely to quickly abandon the Democratic Party. Despite White's warning, neither Roosevelt nor any of his successors managed to pass a federal antilynching law. Despite the fervent hopes of Black America and the passion excited by the New Deal, the country was far from ready to leave the ugliness of racism and the violence it engendered behind.

8

WAR ON TWO FRONTS

Like many big events, the Great Depression was not just a tragedy but an opportunity. Franklin D. Roosevelt took advantage of it to rethink American governance. Everything from the gold standard to the feasibility of a social safety net was on the table, and he seized the chance to shake things up. He created a social security system and banking insurance, reinvigorated the labor movement, and molded the United States into a significantly more enlightened place than it had been prior to the age of Roosevelt. He also made mistakes—and was often guilty of overreach.

In his 1937 State of the Union address, Roosevelt declared that America's task was "to prove that democracy could be made to function in the world of today as effectively as in the simpler world of a hundred years ago." Many thought he should have aimed higher—toward the creation of a democracy that was truly inclusive.

Despite Roosevelt's righteous rhetoric, much of the country, particularly the South, was far from any reasonable concept of democracy. The South's determination to keep Blacks in bondage and the perceived necessity to cater to bigotry endemic among members of the Democratic coalition meant certain lines could not be crossed. Granting southern Blacks the vote and protecting them from lynching were off the table. Also, for Roosevelt and other policy makers, there was a major—indeed overwhelming—distraction as the United States moved inexorably toward war. That war, which had the eradication of intolerance and inequality at its core, cast a fresh light on America's treatment of its own.

———

Since at least September 1938, Europe had been on tenterhooks. When Prime Minister Neville Chamberlain of Great Britain, Chancellor Adolf Hitler of Germany, Prime Minister Benito Mussolini of Italy, and Prime Minister Édouard Daladier of France agreed in Munich to allow Germany to occupy Czechoslovakia, they were unknowingly marching toward the abyss. But before the plunge, there was joy.

Chamberlain was cheered when he arrived at the Munich hotel housing the British delegation; and he was cheered again when he returned to London. Standing before the throng outside his Downing Street residence, Chamberlain proudly compared himself to his nineteenth-century predecessor Benjamin Disraeli. "For the second time in our history, a British Prime Minister has returned from Germany bringing peace with honor," he declared.

Unfortunately, Chamberlain had not achieved peace at all. Germany invaded Poland in September 1939, forcing England and France to declare war. "We sought peace, but Hitler would not have it," grumbled Chamberlain. Two weeks later, Russian troops marched into Poland.

"In the opening phase of the European war, we in America are trying to ride two horses," wrote Raymond Clapper, the Washington correspondent for *Current History* magazine. "We are wishing for and trying to bring about the defeat of Germany. At the same time, we are trying to stay out of the war."

Franklin D. Roosevelt sought to reassure the nervous nation. During a Sunday-night radio broadcast that followed the English and French declarations of war, he pledged, "As long as it remains within my power to prevent, there will be no blackout of peace in the United States." He asked that "partisanship and selfishness be adjourned, and that national unity be the thought that underlies all others."

———

The dream of maintaining neutrality vanished in a flash on the morning of December 7, 1941, when fire rained from the sky over Hawaii. "War broke out with lightning suddenness in the Pacific early this morning when waves of Japanese bombers attacked Honolulu and the great United States naval base at Pearl Harbor," reported the United Press. "The attack broke with such suddenness that at first the identity of the planes [was] not definitely known. But observers soon could plainly see the Rising Sun insignia of Japan on the bombers' wings."

Roosevelt immediately publicly confirmed the attacks on Pearl Harbor and the Philippines. The next day, he asked Congress for a declaration of war. He accused the Japanese of duplicity: "The distance of Hawaii from Japan makes it obvious that the attack was deliberately planned many days or even weeks ago. During the intervening time, the Japanese Government has deliberately sought to deceive the United States by false statements and expressions of hope for continued peace."

The president expressed regret for the lives lost and the damage done to US resources but promised that the United States would triumph: "No matter how long it may take us to overcome this premeditated invasion, the American people in their righteous might will win through to absolute victory. . . . this form of treachery shall never again endanger us." In his radio address the following evening, he explained the stakes:

> We are now in this war. We are all in it—all the way. Every single man, woman and child is a partner in the most tremendous undertaking of our American history. . . .
>
> We are going to win the war and we are going to win the peace that follows.
>
> And in the difficult hours of this day—through dark days that may be yet to come—we will know that the vast majority of the members of the human race are on our side. . . . But, in representing our cause, we represent theirs as well—our hope and their hope for liberty under God.

As the United States mobilized against foreign villains, it also targeted possible threats on US soil. Hours after the Pearl Harbor attack, soldiers converged on Terminal Island in Los Angeles County. The island housed Reeves Field, a civilian airstrip. It was also home to some three thousand Japanese and Japanese Americans. The troops' first act "was the closing of Reeves Fields at 11:30 a.m. as word of the attack on Honolulu was received. . . . [All] leaves were canceled, all visitors were banned and those within the gates were subject to questioning before they were permitted to depart," reported the *Los Angeles Times*.

Many residents were arrested. Hundreds were herded into a wire enclosure for questioning. That was a harbinger of what was to come.

The day after the attacks, dozens of Japanese nationals were rounded up in New York by the FBI. Hundreds more were arrested on the West Coast. The *Los Angeles Times* noted that on the night of

December 8, civilian officials, working under FBI authority, arrested some five hundred Japanese citizens. Attorney General Francis Biddle, who announced plans to arrest many more, specified that only those considered dangerous "to the peace and security of the United States" would be taken into custody.

Meanwhile, the *Atlanta Constitution* reported that all Japanese nationals in Georgia were ordered to stay in their homes and "the guard was ordered doubled at municipal waterworks and defense manufacturing plants" to thwart any attempts at sabotage.

The concern over potentially treacherous Japanese nationals quickly morphed into hysteria over the presence of anyone with Japanese ancestry—particularly on the West Coast. Immediately after the attack, Texas congressman Martin Dies, Jr., the chairman of the House Special Committee on Un-American Activities, launched a frontal attack on Japanese Americans. "We are going to face serious trouble unless we clean up this whole situation at once. The Japanese and Nazis in this country have been working in very close collaboration. We should proceed immediately not only to round up the Japanese aliens known to be potential saboteurs" but also Japanese students, he said.

Shortly thereafter, the House Special Committee on Un-American Activities issued a report claiming that schools for Japanese youths in California and Hawaii were "inculcating traitorous attitudes toward the United States in the minds of American-born Japanese . . . and these language schools were becoming an ever more important arm of Japanese espionage for Japanese citizens residing in the Territories of the United States." The document also accused US-based Japanese civic organizations of "loudly pretending their loyalty toward the United States Government while surreptitiously serving the deified Emperor of Japan."

The *Afro-American* reported that several Japanese nationals, unable to get a White lawyer to take their case, had hired Hugh Macbeth, a Harvard-educated Black lawyer. Macbeth intended to argue "that his clients were not aliens of their own choosing" but had been denied citizenship because of racial restrictions on Japanese naturalization.

Such facts did nothing to staunch the outpouring of anti-Japanese animus, which the House Special Committee on Un-American Activities seemed committed to exacerbating. The committee released a report explaining that because "of their unassimilability and the difficulty of Americans competing with them . . . Japanese immigrants have never been really welcome in the United States." Even Japanese Americans were not truly American: they "do not become assimilated into the lifeblood of this country but remain a part of the Japanese community dominated by their alien parents."

That January, the United Fresh Fruit and Vegetable Association asked the government to imprison people of Japanese ancestry living on the West Coast. The association's president called them "a menace in this country" and predicted that "sooner or later they're going to lead to open shooting." Los Angeles mayor Fletcher Bowron called for relocating Japanese "sufficiently from the Pacific Coast so that their movements could be restricted."

Meanwhile, Congressman Dies was pushing the theory that a Japanese "fifth column" was working toward overthrowing the United States. "The Japanese government's use of its fifth column in the Philippines and in Hawaii is a sample of what the United States can expect from the Japanese fifth column located on our Pacific Coast," declared a report by Dies's committee.

The columnist Walter Lippmann promoted the same xenophobic nonsense, spinning a theory about "imminent danger of a combined attack from within and from without." He urged that Japanese Americans be stripped of their constitutional rights: "Nobody's constitutional rights include the right to reside and do business on a battlefield." Indeed, California Congressman Harry Sheppard believed that those of Japanese heritage no longer had rights. "This is no time to apply civil liberties on questionable citizenship such as the Japs present," he declared.

No evidence was ever produced of a Japanese "fifth column," but the supposed danger was repeatedly invoked as demands for removal of the Japanese grew increasingly urgent.

They were also targeted for violence. A Japanese man in Stockton was shot and killed by an unidentified assailant. Unidentified men invaded a Japanese asparagus workers' camp near Rio Vista, wounding one man and robbing several others. A district attorney in Visalia, California, charged Japanese American gardeners with planting tomatoes that supposedly formed an arrow directing the enemy to an airfield. In Seattle, officials summarily shuttered temples attended by Japanese American Buddhists.

"The temper of the people of the Pacific coast has risen to such a point that it is becoming dangerous for loyal enemy aliens to reside in close proximity to the Pacific Ocean," declared a convention of California county supervisors in February 1942.

In the midst of all the unprovoked hostility, loyal Japanese Americans struggled to make their voices heard. Some fifteen hundred second-generation Japanese Americans formed the Japanese American Citizens League in Los Angeles. At a league meeting, the journalist Larry Tajiri asserted, "We are loyal to the American flag but race hatreds are being stirred up." Kay Sugahara, a produce merchant, blurted out, "If the Army and Navy say we are a menace, let's get out. But if it is merely a question of fighting politicians that would gain favor by hopping on 'those defenseless Japs' we should fight them to the last ditch." Meanwhile, the Japanese American Citizens League announced that its chapters would "continue cooperating with our government."

In the end, it did not much matter what Japanese Americans said or did. Lieutenant General John L. DeWitt, the commanding general of the Western Defense Command, was empowered to treat them however he wanted. And he wanted them gone. "In the war in which we are now engaged racial affinities are not severed by migration. The Japanese race is an enemy race and while many second and third generation Japanese born on United States soil, possessed of United States citizenship, have become 'Americanized,' the racial strains are undiluted. . . . [That] no sabotage has taken place to date is a disturbing and confirming indication that such action will be taken," he wrote in recommendations made public years later by the congressionally appointed Commission on Wartime Relocation and Internment of Civilians.

DeWitt, a native Nebraskan and anti-Japanese bigot, cited as fact what proved to be a hugely consequential lie: that America had evidence of "the existence of hundreds of Japanese organizations in California, Washington, Oregon and Arizona which, prior to December 7, 1941, were actively engaged in advancing Japanese war aims."

On February 19, President Roosevelt issued the anxiously awaited Executive Order 9066, which read:

I hereby authorize and direct the Secretary of War, and the Military Commanders whom he may from time to time designate . . . to prescribe military areas . . . from which any or all persons may be excluded, and with respect to which, the right of any person to enter, remain in, or leave shall be subject to whatever restrictions the Secretary of War or the appropriate Military Commander may impose in his discretion.

"President Acts to End Menace" screamed a *Los Angeles Times* headline. The *Times* noted that DeWitt's decisions would not be subject to appeal. The executive order, officials made clear, would apply only to Japanese—not Germans, Italians, or other enemy aliens. "Of course this is primarily a Japanese problem; a serious Japanese problem," Attorney General Biddle explained to *The Washington Post*.

Not "a single documented act of espionage, sabotage or fifth column activity was committed by an American citizen of Japanese ancestry or by a resident Japanese alien on the West Coast," the wartime relocation commission later reported. But the Japanese were a convenient target. They were "small in number . . . with no political voice."

In a period of weeks, the great relocation began. The Owens Valley Reception Center in Manzanar, California, a former ranching town at the base of the Sierra Nevada, was among the first to welcome the new residents. Nearly a thousand arrived on March 23, the first day of mass relocation. They had been instructed to bring bedrolls and water jugs but no cameras and no guns. The first contingent was male only, with their families scheduled to join them a few days later. As the *New York Times* reported in its "Concentration Camp Special" section:

> The first 500 to arrive, weary but gripped with the spirit of adventure over a new pioneering chapter in American history, drove the 230 miles from the outskirts of Los Angeles in their own cars, paced by highway patrolmen and Army jeeps.
>
> A similar number came by train to the Lone Pine, where buses and trucks met them to carry the evacuees and their possessions the last ten miles to a new reception center rising as if by magic at the foot of snow-capped peaks.

In a separate report, the *Times* noted an upside to the "greatest forced migration in American history"—at least from the perspective of certain residents of Owens Valley, "who showed evidence . . . of a determination to make an asset of an influx of Japanese evacuees" that other communities shunned. "Unbelievers this week began to admit . . . the coming of the Japanese might make this section of the valley . . . a valuable farming area once more."

Meanwhile, the *Los Angeles Times* reassured residents near Santa Anita, whose racetrack parking lots had been pressed into service as a detention center, that "every precaution will be taken to protect the welfare of the surrounding residential areas, and to prevent the interned Japanese from contacting or in any way embarrassing or affecting the lives of Americans living in the areas."

Official actions against enemy aliens of other nationalities were more individualized and selective, as officials assumed that disloyalty had both an ethnicity and a color.

Nonetheless, many Black Americans saw a possible silver lining to the war. Given the stakes and the country's eagerness to be on the right side of the Nazi question, the time might be right, they reasoned, for a reconsideration of the role Blacks could play in the life of the country.

———

Prior to the war, Black efforts at political participation, particularly in the South, had been consistently frustrated. No matter how hard Blacks fought for the right to vote, White southerners determinedly denied it to all but a minuscule percentage of Black residents.

Although Jefferson County, home to Birmingham, Alabama, had a Black population of more than 100,000, only 500 of them were allowed to vote. The situation was much the same throughout the South. Despite the widespread and sincere affection many Blacks felt for Roosevelt, his administration was doing nothing substantial to change that.

In Miami in May 1939, some one thousand Blacks went to polls to vote in a primary election despite direct threats and a public demonstration by a mob in KKK attire. The *New York Herald Tribune* described the demonstration, "in which white-robed men in more than fifty license-shielded automobiles paraded through the Negro section. . . . The paraders burned twenty-five fiery crosses and distributed red-lettered cards reading: 'Respectable Negro citizens not voting tomorrow. Niggers stay away from the polls.' "

In October 1940, the NAACP complained that the Justice Department's new Civil Liberties Division was refusing to protect the rights of Black southerners. "The Department has been overzealous in fighting graft and corruption . . . but it has studiously avoided cases involving the violation of the rights of Negroes protected by the Federal Constitution," read its statement. It highlighted the case of Elbert Williams, a Black NAACP official who had been lynched and whose body had been dumped into a river for leading a voting campaign in Brownsville, Tennessee. "Members of the mob that lynched Elbert Williams can be seen in Brownsville each day going about their work as though they had killed only a rabbit. Tip Hunter, the leader of the mob, recently took office as Sheriff of the county," charged the NAACP.

Alfred Baker Lewis, a White insurance executive and lawyer who served on the board of the NAACP, expanded on the incident in a letter to the *Boston Globe*. After Williams was lynched, wrote Lewis, an associate, Elisha Davis, "was seized from his home by an armed mob late at night and beaten nearly to death, but managed to escape and make his way north." In his flight to safety, Davis was forced to abandon his wife and seven children along with a filling station that he owned. The Reverend Buster Walker, another voting riots campaign leader, escaped death only because he was away from home when the mob seeking to kill him broke down his door. "Both Elisha Davis and Rev. Mr. Walker are literally refugees from America . . . though they had only to go to another section of America to escape," wrote Davis.

Lewis acknowledged that Hitler and Mussolini were "more dangerous enemies of democracy than are members of a lynching mob. . . . But both lynching mobs and Hitler alike are enemies of democracy to the limit of their power."

Lewis had plenty of company among progressive thinkers, who compared Hitler's abuses with those of American segregationists and who thought it absurd to mobilize a racially segregated army to fight fascism and Nazi intolerance or to abuse Black civilians attempting to support the war effort.

Charles Diggs, a Black state senator from Michigan, complained about government contractors barring Negroes from jobs in the defense industry. He cited a *Wall Street Journal* recruitment ad targeting "native white, reliable intelligent labor" for work in Louisiana, Texas, Florida, Michigan, and Mississippi. The *New York Amsterdam News* pointed out that defense contractors were more inclined to hire "enemy aliens" than Black Americans.

In December 1940, Walter White published an essay in the *Saturday Evening Post* titled "It's Our Country, Too," in which he wrote, "The Negro insists upon doing his part, and the Army and Navy want none of him." He acknowledged that under pressure from Blacks, Congress was finally permitting Americans to serve "regardless of race or color"; but it had included a confounding caveat in the legislation by mandating "that no man shall be inducted . . . unless and until he is acceptable to the land or naval forces."

"After considerable research, it seems clear to me that the land and naval forces have not managed to find a way by which Negroes can be 'acceptably' inducted," wrote White. "The bars likewise appear to be up in many of the industrial establishments engaged on defense orders."

As White's article hit newsstands, the *Atlanta Daily World* focused on Jim Crow recruitment practices. In Emporia, Virginia, Blacks attempting to register for military service were ordered to "go to the back door," reported the newspaper. Military facilities should not inflict such practices, common in White private residences, on "potential Negro soldiers who came there to offer their lives," groused the head of the Greenville NAACP, who wondered how a democracy with such morale-destroying practices could effectively take on Hitler.

A. Philip Randolph, the founder and president of the Brotherhood of Sleeping Car Porters, was determined to stop the US government from accommodating Jim Crow. In January 1941, he penned a statement widely reprinted by the Black press proposing a massive march on Washington.

He began with a series of provocative assertions:

Negroes are not getting anywhere with National Defense. The whole National Defense Setup reeks and stinks with race prejudice, hatred, and discrimination. It is obvious to anyone who is not deaf, dumb and blind that the south, with its attitude that the Negro is inferior, worthless, and just simply don't count, is in the saddle. . . .

But the southerners are not alone responsible for the fact that Negroes are being brutally pushed around. The north, east and west are also to blame, because they wink, connive at and acquiesce in this practice of discriminating against Negroes.

Appeals to decency and common sense had failed, and a dramatic show of force was required, argued Randolph.

He proposed that ten thousand African Americans march on Washington in support of a simple proposition: "WE LOYAL NEGRO AMERICAN CITIZENS DEMAND THE RIGHT TO WORK AND FIGHT FOR OUR COUNTRY." Such a demonstration, he declared, "would wake up and shock official Washington as it has never been shocked before. . . . Negroes are not supposed to have sufficient iron in their blood for this type of struggle."

Excitement about the proposal surged through Black communities, which finally had a focus for their pent-up frustration over segregation.

A high-wire game of brinkmanship ensued, with Randolph banking that President Roosevelt would choose to act on his complaint rather than face ten thousand Black Americans collectively denouncing US policy.

By May, excitement had built to such a pitch that organizers were projecting a cavalcade fifty thousand strong. "The spectacle of 50,000 Negroes silently marching through the streets of Washington, behind muffled drums, will become a reality," an organizer told the *Chicago Defender*. By mid-June, Randolph was shooting for a crowd of a hundred thousand, with the confrontation set for July 1. The organizing committee, meanwhile, urged its supporters to plan to march "on their city halls and councils in their respective cities" the week before the big event. "When 100,000 Negroes march on Washington, it will wake up Negro as well as white America. It will stun the government, shock business and astonish organized labor," predicted Randolph in the *Amsterdam News*.

First Lady Eleanor Roosevelt was alarmed at the prospect. According to the *Atlanta Daily World,* she wrote Randolph the following letter, dated June 10, arguing against the march:

> I have talked over your letter with the President and I feel very strongly that your group is making a very grave mistake at the present time to allow this march to take place. I am afraid it will set back the progress which is being made, in the army at least, toward better opportunities and less segregation.

Mrs. Roosevelt went on to argue that any incident resulting from the march might engender bitterness and "even more solid opposition from certain groups than we have had in the past." She understood "that crusades are valuable and necessary sometimes," and was "deeply concerned about the rights of Negro people," but Randolph's approach seemed to be unnecessarily risky.

On June 13, Mrs. Roosevelt met with Randolph and NAACP leader Walter White in New York and asked them to cancel the march. Instead, the organizing committee issued a statement asserting that it had "renewed its confidence in this drive" and was "determined to make the March on Washington the greatest demonstration of Negro mass power for our economic liberation ever conceived."

Shortly after that meeting, President Roosevelt sent a memo to the Office of Production Management, requesting—not ordering—the agency to integrate Blacks into the national defense program. The gesture, apparently aimed at convincing the march committee to stand down, merely strengthened its resolve. Randolph demanded that Roosevelt put forth a measure with "teeth."

The following Wednesday, President Roosevelt welcomed to the White House a delegation of prominent Blacks, including Randolph and White. Secretary of War Henry Stimson and several other administration officials attended.

Roosevelt insisted that the march would anger Whites, who would interpret it as an unwarranted effort by Blacks to force the government's hand. "What would happen if Irish and Jewish people were to march on Washington?" he asked. He answered himself: "It would create resentment among the American people."

Randolph argued that there was "no comparison between a march on Washington by Jews and Irish people and the Negroes. The public knows that the Negroes have justification for bringing their grievances to the President and to present them to the American people."

After the meeting, Randolph and his colleagues declared that the march would proceed.

A week later, Roosevelt signed Executive Order 8802, which instructed government agencies to "take special measures" to eliminate discrimination in defense production work. It also established a committee on fair employment that would investigate allegations of discrimination and take "appropriate steps to redress grievances which it finds to be valid." Upon signing, Roosevelt asserted, "The democratic way of life within the Nation can be defended successfully only with the help and support of all groups within its borders."

Randolph immediately canceled the march. In a national radio address on June 28, he put Roosevelt's action into context: "This is the first executive order which has been issued by a President of the United States [on] behalf of Negroes since the immortal Abraham Lincoln issued the Emancipation Proclamation in 1863." He expressed hope that the sentiment behind the executive order would "help to cleanse the soul of America of the poisons of hatred, antagonisms and hostilities of race, religion, color and nationality."

————

The attack on Pearl Harbor triggered widespread calls for unity from communities across the United States.

The Black press pledged unconditional support but reminded readers of the unfinished work at home. In an editorial headlined "War— And National Unity At Last," the *Norfolk Journal and Guide* declared:

> In this hour of grave crisis the United States can, as has always been true, depend upon the absolute loyalty and devotion of our 12,000,000 Negro-Americans. . . . We crave the opportunity to serve—and we do not crave to serve in the softest places. . . . [We] are realistic enough to know that . . . the dreadful thing that today challenges the United States . . . is more dangerous, more devastating, than anything that could happen under our present way of life. We therefore close ranks and join with fervent patriotism in this battle for America.

The *Chicago Defender* was less magnanimous: "The realization is growing that to fight for freedom in the four corners of the earth and not have it in America is hypocrisy of the rankest kind." The paper demanded that Roosevelt's administration unequivocally denounce discrimination "and give meaning to such a declaration with forthright enforcement of the decree."

In a column for the *Cleveland Call and Post*, Emmett J. Scott, the special adviser on Black affairs to the secretary of war during the Wilson administration, reminded readers that Black loyalty came with expectations: "Negroes are uncomplainingly responding to the call of the colors, willing to serve and sacrifice and die for all we are professing as our war aims." But, Blacks were also "expecting a more generous, a more sincere, finer spirit of liberality and magnanimity on the part of their fellow-citizens than has been their portion in the past."

Despite being engaged in a battle against fascism and prejudice abroad, US leaders made little effort to fight the bigotry that threatened interracial harmony at home. The US military remained racially segregated. Japanese Americans languished in internment camps. And Blacks continued to be denied the vote they had been promised by the Fifteenth Amendment in 1870. Even as US sailors were winning the Battle of Midway in the Pacific and Germany was preparing for mass extermination of Jews at Auschwitz, southern politicians continued to defend the poll tax and other measures to keep Black Americans under control. Blacks insisted that America could and must do better

In 1942, testifying before a Senate subcommittee, John Davis, the national secretary of the National Negro Congress, argued that seeking an end to the poll tax "is not a selfish pleading. It is a task in the successful completion of which every loyal American has an interest as vital to his interest as victory in the war. Enfranchising the Negro voters of the South is a war measure of gravest importance to our country's victory program."

At that same hearing, George Marshall, an economist and the chairman of the National Federation for Constitutional Liberties, asserted that "poll-tax Congressmen . . . preaching the gospels of racism and bigotry" were "Hitler's most cohesive allies in the Congress."

Such warnings were brushed aside by southern congressmen, who saw their way of life as sacrosanct. Prominent among them was John Rankin, whom Marshall referred to as "the Mississippi Apostle of white Anglo-Saxon supremacy."

Rankin was notorious for his outbursts of racist demagoguery. He had accused the author Pearl S. Buck of promoting intermarriage "with the Japs," which would "mongrelize our Western States." He had charged the poet Carl Sandburg with belonging to "that bunch of Communist agitators that are trying to mongrelize America, stirring up race trouble all over the country, and using the Negroes as a smokescreen for their treacherous designs." He had mounted a totally unscientific campaign to segregate the blood of Blacks and Whites donated to American Red Cross blood banks. The policy of treating all blood as equal, said Ranking, was the result of "troublemaking . . . by a radical communistic element that has flooded in . . . from eastern Europe." Despite—or more likely because of—such outrageous behavior, Rankin continued to be reelected throughout the war and afterward, serving sixteen terms, during which he remained a powerful voice for the South.

Not only was Rankin a racist and xenophobe, he was also an anti-Semite who opposed the Nuremberg trials along with providing sanctuary for displaced Jews. In its obituary for Rankin, in 1960, the *New York Herald Tribune* called him "outspokenly anti-Negro, anti-Jewish, anti-Communist and anti-union." But he was also an "outstanding Mississippian" who "denounced 'Jewish war mongers' and ranted against sending 'our boys to die in the bloody hellholes of Europe.' "

That the *Herald Tribune* acknowledged that he was a racist anti-Semite but also considered him "outstanding" says much about American values of the post–World War II period.

The United States was not only victorious in the war but emerged as the dominant world power—the only country with an atomic bomb and, with it, the power to destroy the world. Its might commanded respect. And its take on things, large and small, mattered.

When President Harry Truman, in March 1947, articulated what came to be known as the Truman Doctrine, he spoke to Americans' values and way of life. The American way of life, in his telling, was "based upon the will of the majority, and is distinguished by free institutions, representative government, free elections, guarantees of individual liberty, freedom of speech and religion, and freedom from political oppression."

Despite the fact that many Americans, simply because of their color, were not entitled to representative government, free elections, or freedom from political oppression, Truman's declaration did not strike many people as odd. The United States, along with much of the world, had simply accepted as normal a reality in which freedom for all somehow excluded persons of color. Americans had accepted as both logical and right that a belief in human equality could comfortably coexist with a belief in White superiority. World War II and the fight against Nazism had done nothing to change that. Indeed, it had reinforced it. The United States had won, after all, with a segregated army (notwithstanding the addition, after much agitation, of Black and Japanese American combat units). The United States had won even while confining innocent Japanese Americans to segregated camps. The United States had won even as southern politicians doggedly refused to reject lynching and poll taxes and despite periodic eruptions of racial violence.

One of the more serious disturbances had taken place in Detroit in 1942, when a White mob had attempted to stop Blacks from moving into public housing there. The historian Harvard Sitkoff described the scene in *Toward Freedom Land: The Long Struggle for Racial Equality in America:*

Fiery crosses burned throughout the city. More than a thousand state troopers had to escort 200 Negro families into the project.

Federal investigators warned Washington officials of that city's inability to keep racial peace, and the Office of Facts and Figures warned that "unless strong and quick intervention by some high official, preferably the President, is taken at once, hell is going to be let loose." Nothing was done in Detroit or Washington. Throughout that year Negro and white students clashed in the city's high schools, and the number of outbreaks in factories multiplied.

In 1943, America witnessed the so-called zoot suit riots in Los Angeles. White sailors, abetted by the police, unleashed four days of violence against Latinos and Blacks after a supposed attack on White sailors by gang members of Mexican descent. The sailors were partly motivated "by a desire to defend their racial privilege and stake in the wartime capitalist boom," speculates historian Luis Alverez. The wartime economy had resulted in "increased numbers of underrepresented workers in the shipbuilding and aircraft industries of Los Angeles and elsewhere, white laborers felt their established privilege slipping away. Working alongside Black migrants from the Deep South and second-generation Mexican Americans . . . sparked resentment among many whites" particularly when "African Americans and Mexican Americans worked alongside white women."

Historian Neil Wynn similarly sees a common motivation behind the 240-plus "racial incidents" the United States experienced in 1943: "While some riots predominantly involved whites attacking blacks, in others, such as Harlem, African Americans focused their anger and frustration on property. Each outbreak had its unique causes, but underlying them all was the sense of change brought about by the war. As black Americans demanded more, whites called for less," he observed in the *Journal of Contemporary History*.

———

In 1948, after a visit to West Germany, the NAACP's Walter White produced an account of the trip for the *New York Herald Tribune*: "Here, I have heard again what I had heard during the war in Africa, Europe and the Pacific: 'How dare America call herself a democracy as long as she maintains a white army and a black one and permits . . . racial discrimination at home to continue unchecked,' " he wrote.

A. Philip Randolph again declared war on government hypocrisy with a letter to President Truman demanding an end to racial segregation in the armed services. He formed the League for Non-Violent Civil Disobedience Against Military Segregation and threatened a civil disobedience movement if Congress passed a draft law that sanctioned discrimination in the armed services.

In testimony that April before the Senate Armed Services Committee, Randolph warned that "passage now of a Jim Crow draft may only result in a mass civil disobedience movement along the lines of the magnificent struggles of the people of India against British imperialism" with Blacks demanding "full, unqualified first-class citizenship."

It's unclear what role, if any, Randolph's pressure tactics played in President Truman's thinking; but, on the front page of its July 31 edition, the *Chicago Defender* declared, "In a dramatic and historic move, unprecedented since the time of Lincoln, President Harry Truman issued Monday afternoon two executive orders which doom forever Jim Crowism in the Armed forces of the United States and guarantee equal job opportunities in the Federal government and all of its branches."

The first order mandated an end to unequal treatment "as rapidly as possible, having due regard to the time required to effectuate any necessary changes without impairing efficiency or morale." It also established a President's Committee on Equality of Treatment and Opportunity in the Armed Services. The second order required a policy of nondiscrimination "throughout the federal establishment."

Walter White praised the orders as moving toward the "abolition of segregation," but A. Philip Randolph was not so sure. The equivocal language disturbed him, as it did not specifically abolish segregation but instead ordered "equality of treatment and opportunity."

As the civil rights community debated Truman's intent, reporters pressed the president on his position. At a press briefing on July 29, Truman replied that his order was intended, eventually, to completely eliminate segregation in the armed forces. He dismissed as a misquote a published statement attributed to General Omar Bradley, the army chief of staff, suggesting that the armed forces would not change its policy until "the nation as a whole changes."

Truman's statement was a rejection of the stance taken by southern senators, who insisted that the armed forces need not integrate as long as civilian society remained segregated—which they hoped would be forever. Indeed, they had even proposed legislation that would allow White draftees to decline to participate in integrated units if they wished.

That Truman tried to dance around the issue was no doubt due in part to the approaching presidential election and the uncertainty as to how much government-imposed racial equality White Americans were prepared to accept.

A controversial national poll published by the National Opinion Research Center in 1946 had found that 66 percent of Whites felt that Blacks were already getting a "square deal." Only 28 percent of Blacks agreed. In the South, 76 percent of Whites thought Blacks were being fairly treated.

In light of such strong White sentiment favoring the status quo, Truman was understandably leery of being seen as moving too fast. Nonetheless, Blacks, as Randolph perceived, were fed up with the idea that they should accept being treated as inferior human beings for as long as Whites were uncomfortable with equality.

In August 1978, the *Pittsburgh Courier* published an editorial titled "The Order Mr. Truman Did Not Issue" arguing that in leaving the door open to segregated units, Truman's order had ensured that Black officers would be assigned to such units and thereby generally denied Blacks the possibility of rising in rank above that of commanders of such units:

> Of the score of American nations, the United States is the only one that persists in the wrong-headed and unnecessary policy of racial segregation in its armed forces, yet it is this country which assumes the leadership in carrying democracy to others. If President Truman wants to win an enduring place for himself in American history close to that occupied by the sainted Lincoln, then let him issue another order in his capacity of Commander-in-Chief of the armed forces which will effectively kill the custom and concept of racial segregation.

Whites, for the most part, simply did not accept that formulation—as the NORC poll made clear. From the perspective of most Whites, particularly those from the South, Blacks were already getting exactly what they deserved.

That "truth" could never be pierced by facts (which were easily dismissed) or by moral arguments (since bigots invariably believe that they hold the moral high ground). And that was the crux of the American dilemma. For although World War II proved that the United States was perfectly capable of conquering foreign racists and anti-Semites, it demonstrated, sadly and conclusively, how ill equipped the country was to acknowledge, much less remedy, the bigotry rotting it from within.

9

ENDING AMERICAN APARTHEID

In a fairer world, the civil rights movement would have been unnecessary, as Reconstruction would never have ended as it did—with America giving responsibility for the welfare of "freedmen" to the very people who insisted that they had no rights, to the very people who had nearly wrecked the Union in a futile quest to keep human beings enslaved. But that fairer world was yet to be forged, and the questions that should have been long since resolved were deferred until after the Second World War.

With Nazis as the enemy, a reckoning had become inevitable. How could the world's leading nation, its only real superpower, resolve its own contradictions? In what moral universe was it possible to stand for both democracy and racially restricted voting, to support both equality and bigotry, due process and lynching?

Such questions were at the heart of the so-called Double V Campaign, which assumed that defeating homegrown racism was as important as defeating foreign fascism. That movement had been launched by a letter in January 1942 from James G. Thompson, a *Pittsburgh Courier* reader. *Courier* editors ran the letter on page 3 under a headline reading, "Should I Sacrifice to Live 'Half-American?'"

Thompson made the point bluntly: "Being an American of dark complexion and some 26 years, these questions flash through my mind: 'Should I sacrifice my life to live half American?' 'Will things be better for the next generation in the peace to follow?' 'Would it be demanding too much to demand full citizenship rights in exchange for the sacrificing of my life?['] Is the kind of America I know worth defending? Will America be a true and pure democracy after this war? Will Colored Americans suffer still the indignities that have been heaped upon them in the past?"

Thompson suggested that Americans aspire to a "double victory." He noted that the "V for victory" sign was already on prominent display "in all so-called democratic countries which are fighting for victory over aggression, slavery and tyranny." He suggested that "colored Americans adopt the double VV for a double victory. The first V for victory over our enemies from without, the second V for victory over our enemies from within. For surely those who perpetrate these ugly prejudices here are seeking to destroy our democratic form of government just as surely as the Axis forces."

The *Courier*'s readership rallied around Thompson's idea. Then the largest Black newspaper in America, the *Courier* reported being "inundated with hundreds of telegrams and letters of congratulations, proving that without an explanation, this slogan represents the true battle cry of colored America."

Courier staff artist Wilbert L. Holloway developed the Double V insignia, which featured a graphic of one V atop another, along with the words DEMOCRACY, DOUBLE VICTORY, AT HOME—ABROAD. The newspaper enthusiastically took on the task of producing and distributing Double V pins, stickers, posters, and other paraphernalia aimed at driving home the irony, the insanity, of sacrificing US lives in the fight against racism and anti-Semitism abroad while brutally compelling apartheid at home.

The Double V Campaign was not the only sign that, for many Black Americans, World War II was a turning point. "The nearly ten-fold increase in NAACP membership during the war . . . suggests a dramatic arousal of civil rights consciousness among blacks," suggested the historian Tracy E. K'Meyer. Another concrete sign "of the height-ened activism of black war veterans was the wave of lynchings that greeted them, some while still in uniform, upon their return to the South," observed the legal scholar Michael Klarman.

African Americans were hardly alone in their hunger for funda-mental change. The war had made racist ideologies difficult to defend. Even social scientists "had turned against the idea of higher and lower races—indeed, they threw cold water on race as a meaningful category altogether," noted the legal historian Lawrence Friedman.

Also, the United States no longer existed in relative isolation; it had become the world's preeminent superpower. "In an isolationist era, American race relations conceivably could remain solely an American concern," argued Klarman. "But with the commencement of a life-or-death struggle against the Soviet Union for the allegiance of a pre-dominantly nonwhite Third World, American race relations acquired international implications."

Victims of discrimination were not just emboldened to speak up; they demanded satisfaction in court.

One pivotal case revolved around a California school district's practice of forcing Mexican American students to attend separate but supposedly equal schools. Five fathers filed a class action suit against the Westminster School District (*Mendez et al. v. Westminister School District of Orange County et al.*) on behalf of their children and five thousand other students of Mexican extraction. They argued that discrimination by language and ancestry was prohibited by both California law and the US Constitution.

US District Court Judge Paul McCormick agreed. In a decision handed down in February 1946, he ruled that singling out Mexican Americans violated both state law and federal law. Then he went beyond the law to make a passionate case for integration: "The evidence clearly shows that Spanish-speaking children are retarded in learning English by lack of exposure to its use because of segregation, and that commingling of the entire student body instills and develops a common cultural attitude among the school children which is imperative for the perpetuation of American institutions and ideals." Also, "the methods of segregation prevalent in the defendant school districts foster antagonisms in the children and suggest inferiority among them where none exists."

The school district appealed the decision. In rejecting the school district's arguments, an attorney for the students invoked the ghost of Hitler: "If we accept the premise . . . that a school board can do anything it desires and not be in violation of the Federal Constitution, a board can start segregation with children of Mexican descent, go on with Germans and other national origins and end up by dividing with respect to religion, and we'll have the same situation we had in Germany." The appeal failed and Judge McCormick's order stood.

The month before the California decision, Ada Lois Sipuel applied to the University of Oklahoma College of Law. A twenty-two-year-old honor student, Sipuel was rejected because of her race. Under Oklahoma law, Black students were strictly segregated from Whites. Their designated college was Langston University. If Langston didn't offer the desired curriculum, a Black student had to enroll in a school outside the state.

With an NAACP attorney at her side, Sipuel sought a court order mandating her admission to the University of Oklahoma. The attor-

ney argued that forced segregation amounted to "unlawful discrimination" and was a device for keeping Negroes "in a constantly inferior
position." The Oklahoma courts rejected the argument, and the case
ended up before the US Supreme Court.

In January 1948, the Court delivered a one-page opinion ordering
that the state provide Sipuel with an education "in conformity with the
equal protection clause of the Fourteenth Amendment and provide it
as soon as it does for applicants of any other group."

Sipuel and her lawyers celebrated what they assumed to be a land-
mark victory. "Somebody had to be first. It will be hard but maybe
soon there will be other Negroes with me," commented Sipuel.

Oklahoma, however, had no intention of letting Sipuel into its all-
White law school. With its imprecise language, the Supreme Court
had given the state a considerable amount of wiggle room. Oklahoma
conceded that Sipuel might be entitled to a legal education in the state,
but not necessarily at the University of Oklahoma.

A week after the decision, Oklahoma established a law school specifically for Sipuel as part of Langston University. The Supreme Court
declined to force the state to do more. But as other Black students demanded a graduate education in other fields of study, Oklahoma realized that it could not afford to create separate schools to accommodate
all their needs. So, it passed a new law permitting Blacks to attend
formerly all-White colleges but under segregated conditions, meaning
that Blacks had different times for the snack bar, separate restrooms,
and separate study areas—and were sometimes in separate classes.

The same year the Court decided the Sipuel case, it passed judgment on racial covenants in *Shelley v. Kraemer*. A Black family had
bought a home in St. Louis that they had been unaware was covered by
a racially exclusive covenant drafted by the owners in 1911. For a period
of fifty years, under the provisions of the covenant, only Caucasians
could occupy the property. Blacks and members of the "Mongolian"
race were specifically excluded.

The Court concluded that the restrictive covenants were not, in themselves, unconstitutional. People were free to exclude whomever they wished; but the state could not enforce such agreements since that would violate the Fourteenth Amendment's promise of equal protection.

"Whatever else the framers sought to achieve" with the Fourteenth Amendment, "it is clear that the matter of primary concern was the establishment of equality in the enjoyment of basic civil and political rights," concluded Chief Justice Fred M. Vinson's decision. Three justices—Stanley Reed, Robert Jackson, and Wiley Rutledge—recused themselves, presumably because they owned property covered by such covenants.

Whites in Washington interviewed by *The Washington Post* were dismayed by the ruling. "I'm putting up the for-sale sign tomorrow," declared one homeowner. Another confided, "We did everything we could to keep this block white . . . but now there isn't a thing we can do."

———

In 1950, the Court revisited the issues raised by Ida Lois Sipuel. The plaintiff this time was Heman Marion Sweatt, a Black mailman refused admission to the University of Texas School of Law. Texas responded by offering Sweatt admission to a separate law school that it would create for Black students. On June 5, 1950, the Supreme Court ruled in *Sweatt v. Painter* that the all-Black school was not "substantially equal" to the University of Texas Law School and ordered Sweatt's admission to the then all-White school.

The same day it decided the Sweatt case, the Court also ordered graduate schools integrated at the University of Oklahoma (*McLaurin v. Oklahoma State Regents*). In another case also decided that day (*Henderson v. United States*), the Court refused to rule on the "separate but equal" doctrine but declared it unconstitutional to segregate train dining cars traveling across state lines.

The *Chicago Defender* was exultant: "The United States Supreme Court . . . struck the mightiest blow for freedom and full citizenship of Negro Americans since the Civil War."

Sweatt's story did not end in triumph. From the beginning, he faced incredible pressure. He registered without incident in September 1950, but on his first Friday evening, reported the *Journal of Blacks in Higher Education*, "he found a Ku Klux Klan group waiting for him as he left school, and he headed home immediately after class each day to avoid harm." Although some faculty members were welcoming, others were openly hostile. One "turned his back and doodled on the chalkboard when Sweatt tried to ask a question after class," according to the *Journal*, and another dropped his normal practice of addressing all students by their last name to "avoid having to refer to Sweatt with the courtesy title 'Mr.' "

Sweatt announced shortly after enrolling that he would be unable to complete his studies without financial assistance. The Houston-based NAACP Sweatt Victory Fund responded by raising nearly $10,000. Nonetheless, a year after entering the law school, Sweatt flunked out.

The *Cleveland Call and Post* blamed a "combination of factors," including Sweatt (who had not attended school for more than a decade) being academically rusty, a wife who had opposed his decision to go to law school, and unspecified health problems. He had also faced death threats and been treated as a pariah, including being forced to sit apart from his classmates.

Sweatt's nephew James Sweatt told an interviewer for the *Journal* that his uncle "remembered with bitterness his time at the University of Texas and the harrowing hardships he had to go through. None of these facts, however, were remembered by whites who were there at the time."

Sipuel's story had a happier ending. She graduated, as planned, in

1951 and was honored with a celebration at a local Baptist church in Chickasha, Oklahoma. She passed the bar exam the following year. Sipuel, who in the meantime had married, told an interviewer that she planned to seek work "as soon as my baby is old enough for me to give more time to my profession." She already had offers from three law firms and was "anxious to get into a firm where I can plunge into a practice covering the civil rights field." After working as a civil rights lawyer and as public relations director for Langston University, her alma mater, Sipuel returned to the University of Oklahoma for a master's degree in history before joining the social sciences faculty of Langston. In 1995, three years before her death, she was named to the board of regents of the University of Oklahoma.

———

As the NAACP fought segregation in the courts, it continued, along with its numerous allies, to engage in lobbying and direct action. In January 1950, it chaired a three-day rally in Washington, DC, in support of President Truman's proposed civil rights legislation. More than four thousand delegates representing sixty organizations from thirty-three states converged on the nation's capital for what they called the National Emergency Civil Rights Mobilization. Among the groups represented were the American Federation of Labor, the American Veterans Committee, the Congress of Industrial Organizations, the American Civil Liberties Union, the American Jewish Committee, and the Anti-Defamation League.

Senator Hubert Humphrey keynoted the event. At its first public session, he told the crowd jammed into All Souls Unitarian Church:

> The most vital issue facing the American Congress today is that of civil rights. The preservation of human rights is the para-

mount issue of our generation. . . . The denial of human liberty, the betrayal of democratic ideals, is the sin and the crime of Communism and other totalitarian doctrines. . . .

We weaken our national strength in direct proportion to the number of people that we discriminate against.

On the afternoon of January 17, a delegation from the conference, led by NAACP executive director Roy Wilkins, met with President Truman in the White House. As Wilkins began to speak, Truman interrupted him with "You don't need to make that speech to me. It needs to be made to Senators and Congressmen." Truman promised to press Congress to pass a civil rights program, "even if it takes all summer."

The *Jewish Advocate* described the Washington rally as "the most effective demonstration for civil rights in the history of the long struggle for laws to prohibit discrimination in employment and to outlaw other infringement of civil rights."

The *Baltimore Sun*, however, noted that "Mr. Truman's civil rights program touched off a Southern revolt in the Democratic party two years ago and cost him four Southern States in the election."

———

Even as civil rights legislation stalled in Congress, the human costs of sustaining a Jim Crow South became increasingly apparent. In September 1950, three Black men seriously injured in an automobile accident were taken to Breckinridge County Hospital in Kentucky. Because the hospital did not admit Blacks, the men were left waiting on the floor for more than three hours as the hospital awaited an ambulance from a Black company some seventy miles away.

One of the men, Leroy Foley, died while waiting. The ambulance driver told reporters that the men had received no treatment other than morphine shots: "The blood had not even been wiped from their faces."

The doctor on duty defended the hospital's negligence, saying "We never admit a colored person. But we took the men in and cared for them."

The men's families were later sent a bill for emergency room treatment and for the call to the ambulance service.

Outraged by the hospital staff's behavior, the Progressive Party of Kentucky mounted a campaign to open all hospitals to people of all races. That campaign spawned the Interracial Hospital Movement, a coalition that included some thirty organizations (including church groups, the NAACP, and several labor unions) that met with the governor.

As a result, "the Kentucky General Assembly passed a bill forbidding all licensed medical institutions to deny emergency care to any person on the basis of color or creed. In at least six cities similar citizens movement combatting Jim Crow medical care are under way," reported former first lady Eleanor Roosevelt in her syndicated newspaper column. She also posed a hypothetical question: "Suppose we white people were taken ill in [other] areas of the world and this type of segregation were practiced against us?"

That enlightened people were raising obvious questions did not mean the United States was on the verge of change. But it did mean that for people of intelligence and character, America's monumental hypocrisy on race was getting harder and harder to accept—a fact that unfortunately did not help Harry Moore.

Moore was a Florida NAACP leader whose twenty-fifth wedding anniversary fell on Christmas 1951. That night, as he slept, a bomb went off under his home, killing him and fatally wounding his wife.

The grand jury investigation revealed that floor plans of Moore's home had been shared during a central Florida Ku Klux Klan meeting. No one was ever accused of the crime, but some forty years later the *Orlando Sentinel* reported on confidential FBI documents that identified Orange County KKK members the FBI suspected had been responsible.

The year after Moore's murder, the NAACP posthumously

awarded him its highest honor, the Spingarn Medal, along with a citation praising his courage in opposing segregation at the University of Florida, fighting for Black Floridians' right to vote, and resisting "all the sinister manifestations of racism" festering in his home state.

In Moore's memory, the poet Langston Hughes penned "Ballad of Harry Moore," condemning those who had gone to his door on Christmas night "bearing hate instead of love."

———

Baton Rouge, Louisiana, was also struggling with the quickly evolving racial environment in which Blacks sought ways to ease their oppression without incurring the wrath of Whites. One possible option was to make bus rides less humiliating.

In early 1953, a group led by Reverend T. J. Jemison, the pastor of one of the city's largest Black churches, approached the Baton Rouge City Council to request a change in the law mandating where passengers sat on a bus. Under the current system, the front half of the bus was reserved for Whites and the back half for Blacks, even though Blacks made up roughly 80 percent of bus riders. As a result, buses often cruised along with the Black section packed and Black riders standing, although the White section was virtually empty.

Why not move to a system with Blacks filling seats from the back and Whites taking seats from the front, with all seats open on a first-come basis? asked Jemison. That March the City Council unanimously approved an ordinance approving the new process.

Under the new rules, Negroes were permitted to sit "wherever there was an unoccupied seat," although the law specifically ordered that "no passengers of different races shall occupy the same seat," reported the *Pittsburgh Courier*. The measure was "hailed by both white and Negro citizens," noted the *Courier*. It was not, however, hailed by Baton Rouge's White bus drivers, who preferred that Blacks stand rather than take the seats of Whites who might never show up. The drivers went on strike and remained out for four days. In response, the Louisiana attorney general ruled that the new ordinance violated state law.

Infuriated by the city's flip-flop, Blacks rebelled. Rather than meekly comply with the attorney general's ruling, they boycotted the bus system, with the full backing of Black churches, which raised some $1,000 to subsidize car owners who would provide free rides.

"Baton Rouge this week found itself with a real transportation headache when [the] unwillingness of Negro passengers to be shifted from seat to seat in city buses clashed head-on with Louisiana's travel segregation laws," reported the Norfolk *New Journal and Guide*. City spokesmen acknowledged that virtually no Negroes were riding city buses.

After a week, the City Council collectively blinked and offered a compromise that allowed Blacks to sit wherever they wished except in the two front seats. Reverend Jemison, the head of the United Defense League, agreed to the settlement, although he promised to challenge the segregation laws in the courts.

"Baton Rouge's bus boycott of 1953 was a watershed event in the city, and it proved to be a beginning of an activist national civil rights movement that had up to that point concentrated on legal attacks on segregation rather than direct conflict," wrote Dean Sinclair in *The Journal of the Louisiana Historical Association*. "The ordinance was subsequently challenged in court, but it would take nine years before segregation was eliminated on Baton Rouge's buses," he added.

––––––

The year after the Baton Rouge boycott, Americans witnessed the racial reckoning engendered by *Brown v. Board of Education of Topeka*, the Supreme Court decision that officially outlawed "separate but equal" schools, igniting an epic battle between a South that was determined not to change and a justice system insisting that it must.

The ruling, handed down May 17, 1954, was big news around the world. Chief Justice Earl Warren read the decision aloud to a tense, packed courtroom. It explicitly rejected *Plessy v. Ferguson*, the 1896 Supreme Court ruling in which the Court had justified segregated railway seating by arguing that "social prejudices" could not be "overcome by legislation" and that equal rights could not be secured "by an enforced commingling of the two races."

"If the two races are to meet upon terms of social equality, it must be the result of natural affinities, a mutual appreciation of each other's merits, and a voluntary consent of individuals," declared Justice Henry Billings Brown's decision. Brown assumed that that would never happen, since he deemed Blacks incapable of measuring up to Whites. "If one race be inferior to the other socially, the Constitution of the United States cannot put them upon the same plane," he wrote.

Warren rejected that reasoning root and branch: "We conclude that, in the field of public education, the doctrine of 'separate but equal' has no place. Separate educational facilities are inherently unequal." Also such segregation "violates the Due Process Clause of the Fourteenth Amendment."

Southern politicians reacted with outrage. "For the first time the court admittedly substituted psychology for law and precedents when it came to interpreting the Constitution," fumed Georgia senator Richard Russell.

Congressman John Bell Williams of Mississippi said that the decision would "reverse the gears of orderly process and set the cause of the Negro in the South back 100 years."

Georgia Governor Herman Talmadge accused the Court of reducing "our Constitution to a mere scrap of paper" and announced that Georgia had approved laws "to abolish its public schools in the event of the decision reached today."

Thurgood Marshall, the NAACP's top lawyer, predicted that school segregation would perish within five years. By 1963, conjectured

Marshall, all forms of segregation in America would be nothing but a memory, thanks to the Court's decision. "Free by 63" was the popular slogan that summer at NAACP gatherings.

Eventually people noticed the obvious: that the unanimous decision was exceptionally direct in terms of intent but frustratingly vague about how the goal should be achieved.

The *Brown* decision was actually two decisions involving five separate cases—in South Carolina, Virginia, Delaware, Kansas, and Washington, DC—all of which came collectively to be known as *Brown*. Instead of abolishing segregation straightaway, the justices sought advice on how—and when—desegregation was to come about.

So *Brown* spawned what came to be known as *Brown* II—a decision in May 1955 that provided neither a timetable nor a plan. Instead, it ordered the South—a region filled with the most obstructionist politicians imaginable—to proceed with "all deliberate speed." And it advised the lower courts, which would oversee compliance, to show "a practical flexibility in shaping remedies and a facility for adjusting and reconciling public and private needs."

What exactly did "all deliberate speed" mean? asked Lawrence Friedman, in *American Law in the Twentieth Century*. "This was a cryptic phrase, to say the least . . . . The South took it to mean what they wanted it to mean: obstruct, obfuscate, and delay," with the result that, in many places, Black students were worse off, at least initially, then they had been before the decision came down.

In an article in the *Virginia Law Review* Michael Klarman pointed out that *Brown*

was directly responsible for only the most token forms of southern public school desegregation. In North Carolina, for example, just 0.026% of black schoolchildren attended desegregated schools in 1961 . . . and that figure did not rise above 1% until after passage of the 1964 Civil Rights Act. Likewise in Virginia, a grand total of 208 blacks, out of a statewide school population of 211,000 . . . , were attending desegregated schools as of May 1961; that number had risen to only 1.63% in 1964. Such figures actually would have represented a stunning success by comparison with desegregation rates in the deep South; not a single black child attended an integrated public grade school in South Carolina, Alabama or Mississippi as of the 1962–1963 school year.

Brown did have a huge impact on politics, conceded Klarman. It propelled southern politics far to the right as segregation became exalted over all other issues. In that fraught environment, "men were elected to all levels of public office who were, both by personal predisposition and political calculation, prepared to use virtually any means of resisting racial change. . . . The predictable consequence was a series of violent confrontations between white supremacist law enforcement officials and generally nonviolent demonstrators."

In March 1956, ninety-six southern senators and congressmen signed a "Declaration of Constitutional Principles," published in the *New York Times,* which declared that the Brown decision was a "clear abuse of judicial power," which was "creating chaos and confusion in the states principally affected. It is destroying the amicable relations between the white and Negro races that have been created through ninety years of patient effort by the good people of both races."

In the wake of *Brown*, some of those self-described good people took it upon themselves to form new advocacy groups: the White Citizens' Councils. The new movement was largely ignored by the establishment press, but the *Daily Worker* reported on an organizing meeting in Marengo County, Alabama.

At the meeting covered by the newspaper a state senator told the four hundred prospective members in attendance, "This is a white man's country. It always has been and always will be." He lambasted what he called a Communist plot to make a Negro vice president of America. The head of a council in a nearby county talked up the importance of denying Blacks the vote.

The *Pittsburgh Courier* described the meeting succinctly: "White bigots met last week in this backwoods hamlet in a dogged attempt to maintain white supremacy and wantonly charged that the NAACP 'wants to open the bedroom doors of . . . white women to Negro men.' "

The *Militant* observed that the Citizens' Councils were "uptown Ku Klux Klans" because they counted the "best people" among their members: "bankers, cotton planters, lawyers, officials, etc." Councils existed in at least fifty-three of Mississippi's eighty-two counties, reported the *Militant*. "These Councils were largely responsible for the passage in the recent elections of a voting restriction amendment . . . depriving Mississippi Negroes of what few voting rights they had."

In the journal *Journalism History,* Professor Laura Richardson Walton traces the White Citizens' Councils' beginning to the efforts of a plantation manager near Indianola, Mississippi. Robert "Tut" Patterson, a former Mississippi State University football star who served as a World War II paratrooper, grew angry upon learning of the *Brown* decision. His five-year-old daughter was about to start school, and he was determined to protect her from contact with Blacks. "I, for one, would gladly lay down my life to prevent mongrelization," he wrote in a letter that he sent to several of his friends. "There is no greater cause," he added.

Patterson took it upon himself to convene a meeting of like-minded men in the living room of a friend. They hoped to save their children from integration. They would try to do it through the courts, but if that failed, they were prepared to start segregated private schools. "The first public meeting was held a week later at the Indianola City Hall," wrote Walton.

The organization quickly set up chapters "in every state in the South" and spawned "similar organizations in non-southern states." The membership rosters of chapters in Mississippi "included many of the state's most prestigious and powerful men. By the early 1960s, it developed into a cosmopolitan business operation precisely functioning under the expertise of knowledgeable and respectable men motivated by a burning desire to protect racial integrity and states' rights in the South," Walton concluded.

For such diehards, whose commitment to segregation was undiminished, it would take decades to accept that the age of absolute, unyielding state-sponsored apartheid was over.

10

RAGE, RESISTANCE, AND THE POLITICS OF RESENTMENT

From the mid-1950s to the late 1960s, the United States was a boiling cauldron of racial chaos, with hope, despair, progress, and hate boiling over almost daily. It was a period during which much of White America was forced to concede what Blacks and other people of color had known all along: that its customary treatment of more than one tenth of its population was not just immoral but foolish. During the period between the murder of Emmett Till and the assassination of Martin Luther King, Jr., most Americans accepted (grudgingly, in many cases) that the country was inexorably changing.

Emmett Till was not the first young Black man to be murdered on suspicion of flirting with a White woman. Nor was he the only innocent victim of racially motivated torture. But his death in August 1955 ignited outrage that persists to this day—in part because his mother invited the world to bear witness to what bigoty had done to her son.

For his alleged act of interracial disrespect, Till was kidnapped, stripped, mutilated, murdered, and tossed into Mississippi's Tallahatchie River. His mother, Mamie Elizabeth Till-Mobley, insisted on an open casket at her son's funeral. "Let the people see what they did to my boy," she insisted. And her boy received a sendoff worthy of a head of state. According to the *Chicago Defender*, more than fifty thousand mourners visited the funeral home to pay homage as his body lay in state. Throughout the night people came, forming lines stretching around the block.

Roberts Temple Church of God in Christ, where the service was held, could hold only two thousand. Several thousand more listened to the service over a public address system. Inside, according to the *Pittsburgh Courier*, "One woman fainted at the sight of Emmett's battered remains. Others broke [into] loud and piercing, screaming sobs."

The *Defender* reported, "The boy's face showed evidence of a brutal beating before his murder. Almost all of his teeth were knocked out and the right side of his face was almost unrecognizable. There was a small bullet hole through his temple."

Roughly a month later, on September 23, the two White men accused of Till's murder were acquitted. "An all-white jury took only one hour and seven minutes today to find two white half-brothers not guilty of the murder of 14-year-old Emmett Till, whose alleged wolf whistle at the wife of one of the defendants led to his death. The verdict was received with shouts of approval from a crowd of 500 who had sat through the five-day trial," reported the *Boston Globe*.

The acquittals ignited large demonstrations in Detroit, Ohio, and Alabama as the NAACP headquarters in New York was "deluged with telephone calls and letters offering financial and other assistance," reported the *Cleveland Call and Post*.

———

Later that year, the Montgomery Bus Boycott captured the world's attention. It made the effort in Baton Rouge look like child's play. Montgomery's protestors were not looking for a gentler version of Jim Crow, and they would not give in after a week.

Montgomery was the stage that made Martin Luther King, Jr., famous. It also made clear, in a way no other protest had, how serious Black Americans were about justice. Like the protest in Baton Rouge, it started with a dispute over bus protocol. Rosa Parks was jailed and fined $14 for refusing to give a White man her seat.

The boycott began in December 1955 and went on for a year. King, then only twenty-six and relatively unknown, was the head of the Montgomery Improvement Association and the boycott's public face.

"The Negroes here decided suddenly last December to stand up against Southern Jim Crow." They would no longer abide "paying fares at the front door but having to enter the bus by the rear door to avoid contact with white passengers" or "walking along the outside of the bus—after paying their fares—and being deliberately abandoned by grinning white drivers" or "suffering in silent humiliation epithets from the drivers like 'black ape,' 'black cow' and 'dirty nigger,' " wrote George Barrett of the *New York Times*.

King described the exasperation similarly: "Those drivers talk to us like dogs. . . . Even other white passengers are not above saying, 'Nigger, get up out of your seat,' " he told the *Afro-American* a week and a half into the boycott. At that point, the boycott was estimated to be costing the bus company $3,000 a day. The loss for the year was said to be more than $750,000.

The homes of several boycott leaders, including King, were bombed. After the bombing of a third boycott leader in August 1956, the mayor, a member of the White Citizens' Council, dismissed the bombings as possible publicity stunts concocted by the boycotters. Whites "don't care particularly how the Negroes solve their transportation problems and don't care if the boycott lasts 100 years," he added.

As the boycotters soldiered on, civil rights lawyers awaited a response to a class action suit they had filed in federal district court in February 1956. That June, a three-judge panel ruled that the "separate but equal doctrine" was not in conformance with the law: "We hold that the statutes and ordinances requiring segregation of the white and colored races on the motor buses of a common carrier of passengers in the City of Montgomery and its police jurisdiction violate the due process and equal protection of the law clauses of the Fourteenth Amendment to the Constitution of the United States."

Citing *Brown v. Board of Education of Topeka*, the Supreme Court affirmed the lower court's decision. The Court rejected a "petition for clarification" and denied a hearing to Montgomery and Alabama officials, effectively settling the issue.

Defiant to the end, the Alabama Public Service Commission told transportation companies throughout the state that the ruling applied only to Montgomery and directed them to continue their Jim Crow policies.

Integration of the buses took place on December 21 and generally went smoothly, although the *Christian Science Monitor* reported that a White man had slapped a Black woman after she had left the bus, causing a cut on her lip.

The *Chicago Defender* called the boycott "a national symbol of the new Negro militance of the South" and gravely warned, "The trail to the new freedom for the Negro is strewn with lost jobs, family dislocations, lynchings, burnings, pogroms, beatings, riot, arson, economic squeeze, banishment, blood, sweat and tears."

On Christmas Eve someone fired a shotgun into Dr. King's Montgomery home only hours after King had announced a campaign of passive resistance to gain Blacks equal access to schools and publicly owned recreational facilities. The blast, at around 1:30 a.m., shattered panes of glass but did little other damage.

———

As the Montgomery campaign went forward, so did the effort to integrate public schools and universities. Autherine Lucy, a native of Alabama, had earned a degree in English at Miles College, a Black college in Birmingham, but wanted to study library science at the University of Alabama. She had originally applied in 1952 and been accepted, then rejected, once officials had realized she was Black. Thanks to the NAACP's lawyers and the courts, she was finally admitted in February 1956—although she was denied dormitory and dining privileges.

Shortly after Lucy's arrival, a mob of students gathered outside the college president's mansion and shouted such things as "Are you a nigger lover?" They pelted Lucy's car with eggs and smashed the windows.

Fearing that the violence would get worse, state troopers escorted Lucy from campus. The university expelled her for her safety, as well as "for the safety of other students and . . . faculty."

Lucy was readmitted by court order, but the school expelled her again, charging her with slandering the university in the lawsuit by accusing the university officials of conspiring against her.

The following year, the nation witnessed cruelty in Little Rock, Arkansas, as a mob of White adults cursed and threatened nine Black teenagers attempting to attend Little Rock's Central High. Governor Orval Faubus sided with the mob and ordered the Arkansas National Guard to surround the high school to keep the Black students out. When the governor refused to stand down, President Dwight D. Eisenhower sent in the 101st Airborne Division to ensure the youths' safety.

Prince Edward County, Virginia, took even more extreme measures. After *Brown* was decided, Prince Edward officials swore to use "every legal and honorable means to continue" its segregated practices.

Eventually, the county closed its public schools altogether. For five years, public schools were shuttered. If you were White, that was no big deal; White children could go to Prince Edward Academy, the newly established "private" school. But Blacks, who were barred from the state-subsidized segregated academies, were left out in the cold. Most saw their educational hopes wither—until so-called free schools finally opened in fall of 1963.

In January 1961, a federal district judge ordered the University of Georgia to accept two Black students: Hamilton Holmes, nineteen, and Charlayne Hunter, eighteen. As had become the southern custom, state officials and fellow students made their lives hell. Riots erupted immediately on campus.

As the *New York Times* described the scene, "A howling, cursing mob laid siege late last night to the dormitory in which Miss Hunter was living. The riot raged out of control for nearly an hour before the police broke it up with tear gas and fire hoses." During the riot, "members of the Ku Klux Klan appeared on the scene in mufti to distribute copies of their racist publication, *The Rebel.*"

A day after they began classes, the two Black students were suspended until "it is safe and practical for them to return." They returned to the campus by order of a federal court a few days later, guarded by police detectives. "Peace and quiet prevailed," reported the *Los Angeles Times*.

Air force veteran James Meredith dreamed of attending the University of Mississippi, but "Ole Miss" wanted nothing to do with him. Even so, NAACP lawyers convinced Supreme Court Justice Hugo Black to vacate a local judge's order denying Meredith admission.

On September 20, 1962, the afternoon Meredith was scheduled to enroll, students held a mass demonstration and sang "Glory, glory segregation," to the melody of "Battle Hymn of the Republic."

Meredith arrived around 1:30 p.m. with an escort of federal marshals. He was ushered into a closed-door meeting at the university's Mississippi Center for Continuation Studies with Mississippi governor Ross Barnett, who had arranged to be appointed as a "special registrar."

Twenty-seven minutes later, Meredith reemerged, followed by Barnett, who announced that Meredith's application had been rejected. Students cheered. As the automobile carrying Meredith and his federal keepers pulled off, students made a feeble and unsuccessful effort to block it.

Such shenanigans went on for several days, until President John F. Kennedy and Attorney General Robert Kennedy intervened. A week after his first attempt to register, Meredith arrived escorted by a five-truck convoy of US marshals attired in riot gear. Ole Miss erupted in a five-hour riot that pitted US marshals against students and angry Oxford, Mississippi, residents. When it was over, 2 people were dead, 75 were injured, and more than 150 had been arrested.

By late October, Ole Miss had settled into a semblance of normalcy.

———

So it went across the South as public schools, universities, and local politicians did all within their power to resist integration, risking and ruining countless lives in the process. But Black Americans had reached a limit and were pushing on all fronts—not just for entry to schools and public facilities but for full citizenship, including the right to vote.

In his famous "Letter from Birmingham Jail," Dr. King attempted to explain to White fellow clergy what it felt like for Blacks, who had finally lost patience:

> I guess it is easy for those who have never felt the stinging darts
> of segregation to say "wait." But when you have seen vicious
> mobs lynch your mothers and fathers at will and drown your

sisters and brothers at whim; when you have seen hate-filled policemen curse, kick, brutalize, and even kill your black brothers
and sisters with impunity; when you see the vast majority of
your twenty million Negro brothers smothering in an airtight
cage of poverty in the midst of an affluent society . . . then you
will understand why we find it difficult to wait.

Four months after penning that letter, King led the March on
Washington for Jobs and Freedom.

The march was inspired by A. Philip Randolph, who had so effectively used the threat of Negroes marching on the nation's capital to jolt
President Roosevelt into action before World War II. Randolph helped
organize the new Washington march, along with an array of other
civil rights leaders: Roy Wilkins, the executive director of the NAACP;
John Lewis, the newly named chairman of the Student Non-Violent
Coordinating Committee; Whitney Young, the executive director of
the National Urban League; and James Farmer, a cofounder of the
Congress of Racial Equality. Along with King, the five men became
known as the "Big Six" in civil rights circles.

Unlike President Roosevelt, who had opposed Randolph's March
on Washington, President Kennedy and the Department of Justice
eventually decided to cooperate. Initially, Kennedy thought that the
march would alienate congressional support for his proposed civil
rights legislation, but in a White House meeting in June with Kennedy
and his brother Robert, the attorney general, the march leaders directly
addressed the president's concerns.

As the historian David Levering Lewis recreated that meeting in
King: A Biography, Kennedy told the group he feared that the march
would provoke a backlash in Congress: "We want success in Congress,
not just a big show at the Capitol. Some of these people are looking for
an excuse to be against us. I don't want to give any of them a chance to

say, 'Yes, I'm for the [voting rights] bill, but I'm damned if I will vote for it at the point of a gun.' "

Randolph responded, "The Negroes are already in the streets. It is very likely impossible to get them off. If they are bound to be in the streets in any case, is it not better that they be led by organizations dedicated to civil rights and disciplined by struggle rather than to leave them to other leaders who care neither about civil rights nor nonviolence?"

King directly countered Kennedy's concern that the march might be ill timed, using language almost identical to that he addressed to southern White religious leaders in "Letter from Birmingham Jail": "Frankly, I have never engaged in any direct-action movement which did not seem ill-timed. Some people thought Birmingham ill-timed."

"Including the Attorney General," agreed the animated and amiable President Kennedy.

———

What most impressed those who witnessed the August 28 rally in Washington was "the speech." King delivered the oration of a lifetime, one that sent chills down the spine and evoked wonder; a speech that articulated not only his dreams but the dreams of Black people going back generations, going back virtually to the arrival of the first ships from Africa; a speech that articulated the desire, never met, of a people to be treated with the simple dignity due to fellow human beings, to be recognized not just for their color, but for who they were and what they could be. It was a cry not just of pain but of anger, of anguish, of impatience with the dishonesty and impertinence of those who said "Wait" when they meant "Never."

"There are those who are asking the devotees of civil rights, when will you be satisfied?" King ticked off the list, building to a crescendo:

We cannot be satisfied as long as the Negro's basic mobility is from a smaller ghetto to a larger one . . . as long as our children are stripped of their selfhood and robbed of their dignity by signs stating 'for whites only' . . . as long as a Negro in Mississippi cannot vote and a Negro in New York believes he has nothing for which to vote. . . . And we will not be satisfied until justice rolls down like waters and righteousness like a mighty stream.

The *Chicago Defender* printed the speech and told its readers, "Rarely has history witnessed a more moving, dramatic or eloquent moment than the hour when America's foremost civil rights leader, Rev. Dr. Martin Luther King, Jr., delivered his brilliant address on the steps of the Lincoln Memorial with the brooding countenance of the Great Emancipator looking down on the 300,000 people assembled." The speech, it added, "is a historical document. It is a declaration of brotherhood and hope you will want to save forever."

New York Times columnist James Reston wrote that until King spoke, "the pilgrimage was merely a great spectacle. . . . But Dr. King brought them alive in the late afternoon with a peroration that was an anguished echo from all the old American reformers."

Despite King's urgent oratory and the coming together of hundreds of thousands of people in the name of freedom, Dixiecrats simply weren't interested in supporting civil rights. If anything, the march, as Kennedy had feared, stiffened the spines of southern senators hoping to bury the president's proposed legislation.

In September, the *Hartford Courant* reported that the civil rights bill seemed "doomed" in the Senate by the threat of filibuster: "The key question, as it has always been on civil rights, is how to get 67 votes. . . . It seems apparent that the 67 votes are not available."

In November, *Newsday* headlined its report "JFK Concedes the Obvious: Two Key Bills Dead for Now." The story acknowledged that the administration's tax and civil rights bills "were hardly breathing and hope that they will win passage before the current session ends Jan. 3 has been abandoned."

On November 22, 1963, everything changed.

While in Dallas, in a motorcade accompanied by ex-governor John Connally, President Kennedy was assassinated. "When the shots were fired about 1:30 p.m. and the Chief Executive slumped forward, Mrs. Kennedy turned . . . and cried, 'Oh, no.' She tried to cradle his head in her arms as the car sped for Parkland Hospital, where Mr. Kennedy died about an hour later," reported the Associated Press.

Lyndon B. Johnson was sworn in at 3:39 p.m. on Air Force One at Love Field Airport outside Dallas. In an address to a joint session of Congress five days after taking office, he declared, "The greatest leader of our time has been struck down by the foulest deed of our time. . . . And now the ideas and the ideals which he so nobly represented must and will be translated into effective action." No eulogy "could more eloquently honor President Kennedy's memory than the earliest possible passage of the civil rights bill for which he fought so long," he said. "We have talked long enough in this country about equal rights. We have talked for one hundred years or more." It was time, he said, to "write the next chapter."

Southern politicians were not moved. Senator Richard Russell of Georgia commented, "This package is not a civil rights bill. . . . It will destroy more than it will establish." Senator Allen Ellender of Louisiana was even more dismissive: "I don't think it will do him a bit of good no matter how he shouts about it. It's strictly political."

In his State of the Union address on January 8, 1964, Johnson declared "war against poverty," promoted "a world made safe for diversity," and pushed strongly for his civil rights bill: "Let this session of Congress be known as the session which did more for civil rights than the last hundred sessions combined."

That June, for the first time in its history, the Senate imposed cloture to vote on a civil rights bill. "In most of the efforts to limit civil rights debates since the cloture rule was adopted in 1917, the Senate was unable even to muster a majority, much less than the required two-thirds approval," observed Associated Press writer John Chadwick.

The bill passed the Senate 73 to 27 on June 19, with Southern Democrats voting overwhelmingly against it. Johnson declared, "No single act of Congress can, by itself, eliminate discrimination and prejudice, hatred and injustice. But this bill goes further to invest the rights of man with the protection of law than any legislation in this century." He added that the task now facing the nation was "to reach beyond the content of the bill to conquer the barriers of poor education, poverty, and squalid housing which are an inheritance of past injustice and an impediment to future advance."

———

Another impediment to progress was the South's practice of methodically and insistently denying Blacks the right to vote. In the minds of many southern politicians, the Fifteenth Amendment had been a tragic mistake. Voting was a privilege they felt most Blacks didn't deserve and must not have.

By 1965, Blacks were fed up with that attitude and the policies that it spawned. Some were prepared to give their lives to change it.

Martin Luther King, Jr., and his associates had always known that despite their commitment to nonviolence, the battle for rights would at times be bloody. Nonetheless, they nonviolently fought on—never more courageously than in Selma, Alabama, on March 7, 1965, which would go down in the history books as Bloody Sunday.

That solemn Sabbath, the full power of the ruthless state of Alabama came down on the civil rights movement, raining cruelty and wrathful anger on marchers just as they began bowing to pray on the Edmund Pettus Bridge, which had been named for a Confederate general. For the crime of insisting on fairness and adherence to the Constitution, they were beaten by mounted state troopers wielding clubs.

In his memoir, *Walking with the Wind: A Memoir of the Movement*, John Lewis, one of the march leaders, wrote:

> The troopers and possemen swept forward as one, like a human wave, a blur of blue shirts and billy clubs and bullwhips. We had no chance to turn and retreat. There were six hundred people behind us, bridge railings to either side and the river below.
>
> I remember how vivid the sounds were as the troopers rushed toward us—the clunk of the troopers' heavy boots, the whoops of rebel yells from the white onlookers, the clip-clop of horses hooves hitting the hard asphalt of the highway, the voice of a woman shouting, "Get 'em! *Get* the niggers!"

Lewis himself was clubbed and almost died. "I didn't feel any pain, just the thud of the blow, and my legs giving way."

Images of the display of official brutality were broadcast internationally and resuscitated the effort to pass a voting rights bill.

On March 15, a week and a day after the attack on the Edmund Pettus Bridge, President Johnson explained to a joint session of Congress the lengths that the South went to in order to deny Blacks the vote:

> The Negro citizen may go to register only to be told that the day is wrong, or the hour is late, or the official in charge is absent. And if he persists . . . he may be disqualified because he did not spell out his middle name, or because he abbreviated a word on the application. And if he manages to fill out an application, he is given a test. . . . He may be asked to recite the entire Constitution, or explain the most complex provisions of

state law. . . . the fact is that the only way to pass these barriers is to show a white skin.

Johnson announced that he was sending legislation to Congress later that week that would strike down such blatant restrictions. He pointed out that the civil rights bill Congress had passed had been stripped of the guarantee of voting rights. This time, he said, must be different: "We ought not, and we cannot, and we must not wait another eight months before we get a bill. We have already waited 100 years and more, and the time for waiting is gone."

Provocatively, intentionally, and to enormous applause, Johnson echoed the language of those leading the fight for civil rights. "It's not just Negroes, but really it's all of us who must overcome the crippling legacy of bigotry and injustice. And we shall overcome." He repeated the phrase later as he talked about the ills of poverty, disease, and ignorance, solemnly ending the litany with—and emphasizing each word: "*We shall overcome.*"

That night Johnson sent a written message to Congress imploring that it eliminate stratagems used to deny Blacks the vote—including using inconsequential "errors" as a pretext to reject ballots and requiring the passing of subjectively administered "tests." It had become clear, he pointed out, that "prompt and fair registration of qualified Negro citizens cannot be achieved under present" circumstances. He was requesting legislation that would establish a consistent standard for voter registration and provide power to federal officials to make sure that voting rights were not denied.

What that meant in practice was that literacy tests, testaments of moral character, and other such provisions would be eliminated, poll taxes would be regulated, voter intimidation would be outlawed, and several "low-turnout" states (where voting was presumably suppressed) would receive special scrutiny. They would not be permitted to change their voting procedures without the permission of the federal government.

Several southern senators immediately rejected the measures as illegal. Louisiana senator Allen Ellender claimed that the proposed bill was unconstitutional and vowed to talk "as long as God gives me breath" to oppose it.

Senate majority leader Mike Mansfield vowed to see the bill through to passage, swearing to keep the chamber in recess over the Easter break if necessary.

House Judiciary Committee chairman Emanuel Celler opened hearings before the committee by declaring "Recent events in Alabama, involving murder, savage brutality, and violence by local police, state troopers, and posses have so aroused the Nation as to make action by this Congress necessary."

The bill passed the Senate on May 26 and the House on July 9. President Johnson signed it into law on August 6, five months after Bloody Sunday. During the signing ceremony in the President's Room of the Capitol, he remarked, "Three and a half centuries ago the first Negroes arrived at Jamestown. . . . They came in darkness and they came in chains. And today we strike away the last major shackle of those fierce and ancient bonds." He pronounced the new law "one of the most monumental laws in the entire history of American freedom."

Congress was not yet done. On October 3, Johnson signed the Immigration and Nationality Act of 1965, finally rejecting the racist assumptions and language that had guided American immigration and naturalization policies since 1790, when naturalization was limited to persons who were free and White. The so-called national origins language was gone, or would be after a three-year period, to be replaced by a concept of family reunification, with race or ethnicity no longer a factor.

The bill did not work out exactly as legislators had anticipated. As I observed in *A Nation of Strangers: Prejudice, Politics, and the Populating of America*:

> Knowing that most Americans hailed from European stock, legislators had assumed that the generous family numbers would almost all go to Europeans; but an unforeseen flood of Asian refugees (who, once settled, could sponsor family members as regular immigrants) would eventually result in numbers intended for Europeans increasingly going to Asians, and the good feelings that had swept through Congress as the 1965 statute gathered steam—when all assumed that the egalitarian new law was little more than a generous gesture—would gradually give way to grave concern.

There was also significant immigration from Mexico and Central and South America, which, to the distress of some, noticeably altered the United States' ethnic mix.

———

Many Americans responded to the changes with anger and resentment, which only grew as the ethos of nonviolent resistance was challenged by rage and urban riots. One after another, largely Black neighborhoods—in Watts, Newark, Chicago, Washington—went up in flames. And in the volatile mix of White resentment and Black frustration, some politicians saw opportunity.

Richard Nixon and George Wallace both realized that catering to White grievance could be the key to electoral success. The election of 1968 pitted the promise of racial reconciliation and the Great Society, as embodied by Hubert Humphrey, against the incitement of White resentment, as stirred up by Nixon and Wallace.

Wallace, a third-party candidate representing the American Independent Party, was the voice of the old, segregated South. "I'd like to appeal to the soul of the South so we can join together and go out to the rest of the country and win," he told a receptive audience in New Orleans. In Atlanta, he defiantly declared, "[Northerners] may call us rednecks, but we're going to show them there are still a lot of rednecks in this country."

At a rally in Missouri, he attacked both Nixon and Humphrey for supporting the civil rights movement: "Mr. Nixon said, 'It's a great movement. It's constitutional, yessiree,' " . . . "Mr. Humphrey said, 'I'd lead a revolt.' And now they all stand saying, 'We've got to have law and order in this country.' "

In Little Rock, Arkansas, he reminded the audience that Nixon had been vice president when Eisenhower had sent in troops to integrate Central High: "When the national Republicans come down here and ask you to support them, you ask them if they're going to give your schools back to you." He also accused Nixon of falsely promising not to shove anything down their throats: "The national Republicans have already jammed everything down our throats there is to jam."

Nixon did not pretend to be a racial healer, but his appeal to prejudice was not nearly as blunt as Wallace's. He cloaked it in talk about being tough on crime and especially tough on Black rioters. "I pledge that a Nixon administration will make it a first order of business to sweep the streets of Washington free of these prowlers and muggers and marauders," he told voters in Chattanooga. During a radio address in early November, he claimed that Humphrey was "giving aid and comfort to those who are tearing down respect for law across the country." He accused Humphrey of being irresponsible in his language about racial conflict: "He does not seem to grasp that when a high officeholder—in the midst of a summer of racial violence—says that if he lived in a slum he could lead a 'mighty good revolt' himself, he provides encouragement and rationale for those who are already revolting violently."

Humphrey fought back by calling out racism and appealing for unity. In Knoxville, Tennessee, he said of Wallace, "He stands, and he has always stood, as the apostle of hate and racism. . . . Today some of his political managers and even some of his presidential advisors are drawn from the ranks of the Ku Klux Klan, the White Citizens' Councils, the John Birch Society, the armed Minutemen, or groups dedicated to the promotion of anti-Semitism. His Georgia state chairman . . . was formerly national president of the White Citizens' Councils."

In Little Rock, Humphrey encouraged Central High students to forgo bigotry: "Let's let these people that preach prejudice, let's let them know we're going to have nothing to do with them, and let's let Mr. Nixon know that he can't get by straddling." In Kansas, he pleaded, "Help me heal the wounds in this country. We must put down the voices of bitterness and hatred that divide us."

The establishment press generally gave Nixon a pass on his pandering to southern-baked racism. The columnist Joseph Alsop was among the few who acknowledged Nixon's "Southern strategy" and his "covert appeals to Wallace voters."

In an interview many years later with *Harper's* magazine writer Dan Baum, John Ehrlichman, Nixon's domestic policy adviser, made clear that Nixon's appeal to White racism was fully intentional:

The Nixon campaign in 1968, and the Nixon White House after that, had two enemies: the antiwar left and black people. You understand what I'm saying? We knew we couldn't make it illegal to be either against the war or black, but by getting the public to associate the hippies with marijuana and blacks with heroin, and then criminalizing both heavily, we could disrupt those communities. We could arrest their leaders, raid their homes, break up their meetings, and vilify them night after night on the evening news. Did we know we were lying about the drugs? Of course we did.

Race, of course, was far from the only issue in the campaign. Indeed, for the most part, it hovered just beneath the surface, out of clear sight but very much on people's minds. The more open debate was about the United States' involvement in Vietnam, from which Humphrey, as Lyndon Johnson's vice president, could never hope to distance himself.

———

In a rational society, both Nixon's and Wallace's racial politics would have been rejected as the pandering to prejudice that they clearly were. The idea that a major party candidate such as Humphrey was in favor of riots and crime is nonsensical. That Nixon could make political hay out of such assertions says more about the political appetites and perceptions of the American voting public of the day than it says about reality.

Nonetheless, the pandering worked magnificently. Taken together, the candidates of law, order, and bigotry won overwhelmingly. Wallace took five states, all in the South: Alabama, Arkansas, Georgia, Louisiana, and Mississippi. Of the southern states, only Texas went to Humphrey. The rest went to Nixon. Humphrey won Minnesota, Michigan, and several states in the East. Nixon swept the rest of the country, winning an Electoral College victory and a plurality of the popular vote. Nixon and Wallace together won 54 percent of the popular vote. White, formerly Democratic southerners, who had spent decades violently resisting integration and lynching Blacks who dared to demand equality, had become Republican champions of "law and order."

Although the race-baiting campaign was the instrument of Nixon's political resurrection, for the Republican Party it represented something different altogether: it was a major step away from the values of Lincoln and into the mire of racial grievances and irrational animosity.

11

SELLING SOAP, FALSEHOODS, AND POTENTIAL PRESIDENTS

Nixon was hardly the first politician to market himself by employing misdirection, by focusing on a theme whose subtext was more powerful than its text, by generating an emotional response that left little room for reason. He was simply demonstrating his mastery of advertising, which is the business of profiting from emotional needs and peddling products that aren't what they seem.

We accept as a matter of course that when we read newspaper ads, watch TV, or peruse the internet, we will ingest a steady stream of misinformation; that we will be lied to, cajoled, perhaps even cheated by people who use our emotions to confuse our minds. Such is the nature of the business and the reality of a culture that embraces it.

How did we get to the point where politicians are sold like products and truth no longer matters?

Both advertising and the US presidency have evolved hugely in the nearly two and a half centuries of the republic's existence—an evolution that has brought them closer together in fascinating and frightening ways. They have both mastered the art of harnessing and manipulating emotions. And the president has become a product, no less so than an automobile or wristwatch—as the presidency grows more powerful and less responsible.

In the *Lost Soul of the American Presidency: The Decline into Demagoguery and the Prospects for Renewal*, Stephen F. Knott observed that our presidency is far from what the Founders imagined: "The American president was intended . . . to serve as the nation's chief of state, as its symbolic head, not a partisan leader." An office "envisioned by George Washington and others as a source of national pride and unity has devolved into a force for division and discord." The Founders' presidency was one of "sober expectations" that "did not pander to or manipulate the public" and that "was loath to implement the majority will at the expense of political, racial, and economic minorities." Knott believes that as early as Thomas Jefferson's tenure, the presidency began to shift "from its intended role."

In *The Selling of the President 1968*, published in 1969, Joe McGinnis documented just how much things had shifted; how debased, in his opinion, the modern presidency had become—at least as viewed from the vantage point of the Nixon campaign. Both politics and advertising, he argued, are con games: "It is not surprising, then, that politicians and advertising men should have discovered one another. And, once they recognized that the citizen did not so much vote for a candidate as make a psychological purchase of him, not surprising that they began to work together."

The practice of promoting the president as product and prophetic savior did not originate with Nixon. Major General Leonard Wood, a former army physician, had won the Medal of Honor for action in the Apache Campaigns during the so-called Indian Wars, commanded a

Rough Riders regiment in the Spanish-American War, served as War Department chief of staff during World War I, and spent four years as military governor of Cuba. He decided to cap his career as president of the United States. He entered the 1920 Republican primary and sought help from a master marketer. William Cooper Procter (the Procter of Procter & Gamble, which manufactured Ivory soap) agreed to be chairman of his election campaign. The idea was for Procter to sell Wood as successfully as he sold his soap.

"Our theory of the campaign was based upon publicity, and the great bulk of our expenses have been for that purpose," Procter told the Senate subcommittee in charge of campaign finance. "Perhaps I have placed undue stress upon publicity, from my business experience," he conceded, adding that between 65 and 70 percent of Wood's campaign expenses had been for promotion, largely for pamphlets and newspaper ads.

In his seconding speech for Wood at the Republican National Convention, Kansas governor Henry J. Allen presented the general as a successful businessman who possessed the "initiative and the prophetic wisdom to guide us" at a moment when the nation required competent leadership. The stated rationale behind Wood's candidacy was strikingly similar to the argument that the Donald Trump campaign would make nearly a century later.

Wood almost succeeded; he led through the first four ballots, but the nomination ultimately went to Ohio senator Warren G. Harding, who earlier had seemed all but out of the race. Harding became the United States' twenty-ninth president.

Procter's methods burst back into the news in 1923 as a result of a suit Procter filed against Wood's campaign treasurer seeking partial repayment of money he had poured into the campaign.

Various supporters testified that Procter had viewed running a presidential campaign much as he viewed a product launch. Herbert L. Satterlee, a wealthy corporate lawyer, explained in his deposition that it had been Procter's plan "to sell the candidate to the people just as if he were an unknown new proprietary article or a useful appliance or invention. He did not place much importance on mass meetings, parades, or speeches by the candidate. He thought the time had passed for all that and that up-to-date business methods must be employed."

The ultimately failed effort for Wood didn't discourage others from following his approach; it just inspired them to get better at it.

By the 1960s, political advertising had become an essential component of presidential campaigns. The 1964 anti–Barry Goldwater ad featuring a young girl picking the petals off a daisy as an atomic bomb counts down in the background is still considered among the most effective ads of all time.

When Richard Nixon ran for president in 1968, the *Wall Street Journal* reported a huge uptick in political advertising. The *Journal* estimated that spending on political radio and TV advertising would total well over $50 million for the year, up from $34.6 million in 1964. Such advertising, observed the *Journal*, consumed the lion's share of total campaign expenses.

As Stephen Knott contended, candidates in the Founders' era were, no doubt, anchored in more honorable values than those who are typically running today. It's impossible to imagine George Washington promoting himself as a "bull in a china shop," as did Donald Trump in 2020. "President Trump's not always polite. Mr. Nice Guy won't cut it. He does it his way, not the Washington way, but Donald Trump gets it done," declared the bull in a china shop ad.

But even had George Washington been inclined to broadcast such an unrefined ad, he could not have done so—for the obvious reason that broadcasting was not yet invented. Indeed, neither was advertising, certainly not as we understand it today. Mass marketing campaigns were not possible, in any meaningful sense, without mass media, and the old world had none. Mass media were far in the future when the Founders gave birth to a new nation.

The world's first English-language newspaper, generally referred to as the *Weekly News*, debuted in London in 1622. The first known advertisement appeared a quarter of a century later in another London weekly, *Perfect Occurrences*. The ad was not what we usually think of as an ad today. It was an endorsement disguised as a news story (what we now call an advertorial) for a book titled *The Divine Right of Church Government*. The ad claimed that the book was popular among "sundry eminent" London ministers and urged readers to buy a copy at "Stationers Hall and at the Golden Fleece in the Old Change."

Initially, the American colonies had no newspapers. As the historian Sidney Kobre pointed out, travel was difficult, the postal service was atrocious, and commercial establishments were sparse. But by the late 1600s, things had changed: roads were better, postal service was more reliable, and seaports were thriving, along with small retailers.

In 1690, Benjamin Harris took advantage of the more favorable environment to launch *Publick Occurrences Both Forreign and Domestick* in Boston. His newspaper was short lived, though not for lack of interest. The colonial authorities shut it down after one issue because Harris had not obtained a license to publish it. They also objected to some of his content, which included an article unflattering to both the French royal family and the British military.

Other publications filled the void. First among them was the *Boston News-Letter*, founded in 1704 by Boston postmaster and bookseller John Campbell, which carried what is acknowledged to be the first paid advertisement in an American newspaper. It was seeking a buyer for a plantation in Oyster Bay, New York, that had a kitchen, a workhouse, and twenty acres of cleared land.

By the 1820s, some six hundred newspapers were circulating throughout America. Central as newspapers were to the new nation's evolving sense of identity, they were not particularly accessible to the masses. Subscriptions, which might cost ten dollars a year, were beyond the reach of ordinary Americans. That was about to change.

In Boston in 1830, Lynde M. Walter started the *Daily Evening Telegraph* and set a subscription rate of only four dollars a year. That same year, Christopher Columbus Conwell founded a penny newspaper named *The Cent* in Philadelphia. The publication lasted only a few weeks, but other people quickly adopted the idea.

In September 1833, the New York printer Benjamin Day and his associates launched the *New York Sun*. Although other papers were selling for six cents, the *Sun* charged a penny. Its self-declared mission was "to lay before the public, at a price within the means of every one, ALL THE NEWS OF THE DAY, and at the same time offer an advantageous medium for advertising."

At the time, New York's eleven daily newspapers had a combined circulation of less than 30,000. Within months, the circulation of the upstart *Sun* reached 5,000. By 1845, the *Sun* had a circulation of nearly 43,000—"The largest circulation of any daily newspaper in the United States," observed the *Baltimore Sun*. A few decades later, its circulation had climbed to roughly 150,000. The penny press had "transformed the daily newspaper from a narrowly focused and sparsely distributed publication to a broad-based, mass-produced medium," wrote the historian Donald K. Brazeal.

The amazing growth was a function not just of the paper's low price but of its often sensational content. In 1834 and 1835, the *Sun* devoted countless pages to "Matthias the Prophet," a carpenter who represented himself as "the Spirit of Truth" and led rituals that included nude public bathings, which purportedly returned believers to a state of spiritual innocence, making them "virgins of the garden." Matthias also claimed to have risen from the dead and somehow embodied "the spirit of Jesus of Nazareth." He was indicted for (and ultimately exonerated of) murdering a man he was accused of having embezzled.

The Matthias the Prophet story was based on truth, but the penny press was not above perpetrating flat-out hoaxes, as it demonstrated in August 1835, when the *Sun* devoted a seven-part series to humanlike inhabitants supposedly spotted on the moon by a noted British astronomer. According to the stories, the moon, whose atmosphere was similar to ours, housed mountains, trees, and various inhabitants: bisonlike animals, horned bears, tiny zebras, flying man-bats, and beaverlike creatures that walked upright and used fire.

An editorial in *Family Magazine* in April 1835 captured the concern and ambivalence the penny press evoked among some thoughtful Americans: "It will enable thousands, nay, millions, who have not heretofore enjoyed access to the daily news, now to gratify themselves in this respect. The consequence will be, that good papers of this description will obtain a circulation altogether unparalleled in the history of the daily press." The editorial fretted about the power such mass circulation newspapers would inevitably accrue. Such power, warned the magazine, could be dangerous, especially if newspaper owners lost their "moral bearing" and catered to "basest passion and prejudices."

It apparently did not occur to the editors of *Family Magazine* that another potential source of power had been tapped by the mass circulation press: the power of advertising. Indeed, the very existence of the penny press, the ability to sell newspapers so cheaply, depended on someone other than readers paying most of the costs. And the obvious someone was people with products and services to sell.

Prior to the emergence of mass media, advertising's impact was severely limited. After that, it was essentially boundless.

The *Baltimore Sun* spelled out the new reality in 1839:

No profit is made on the sale of papers, but in consequence of the cheapness, which carries them into almost every family, a well conducted paper commands a vast amount of advertising patronage at living cash prices. For all kinds of advertising that is desirable to convey to the mechanics, the traders, and the laborers, a penny paper is the most useful, and in fact the only proper vehicle.

The penny press model—with advertising paying the lion's share of the newspaper's costs—was eventually adopted by virtually all newspapers, creating an odd marriage of convenience in which a medium supposedly dedicated to truth was financed by a business largely built on lies.

———

The advertising industry, of course, did not suddenly materialize full blown. "Although the first American advertising agency was founded in 1841, their original function was simply to broker space in newspapers and magazines for commission," observed the historian Daniel Navon. Over the years, their role grew, and agencies came to specialize in seduction through salesmanship. They sold the dream that particular products and particular brands could ensure health, acceptance, and happiness.

The way was paved by such legendary branders as Thomas J. Barratt, an Englishman widely considered the founding father of the modern advertising industry. Barratt's rise to fame began in 1887. After acquiring the rights to John Everett Millais's famous painting of his grandson staring in wonder at a floating soap bubble, Barratt inserted a bar of Pears soap into the image and built an advertising campaign around it. Such branding became the essence of advertising.

"In the early 1800s, soap was just soap. Like biscuits or nails, it came in barrels, and to get some, you told the store clerk, 'Two bars of soap, please.' By the late 1800s—nudged by Barratt's advertising—you might specify Pears' Soap," observed Richard and Joyce Wolkomir in *Smithsonian Magazine.*

Soap was no longer just soap. The right soap not only made you clean; it conferred a certain innocence and youthful beauty and ensured your acceptance into polite society.

It was not only soap that, through advertising, acquired almost magical qualities. Patent medicines, promoting bogus cures for assorted ailments, were even more conspicuously touted. The promotion of such quackery became so egregious that it eventually spawned several journalistic exposés. The most notable was a series of articles, "The Great American Fraud," by Samuel Hopkins Adams in *Collier's Weekly* in October 1905. The series began with a blunt assertion: "This . . . series . . . will contain a full explanation and exposure of patent-medicine methods, and the harm done to the public by this industry, founded mainly on fraud and poison. . . . The object of the series is to make the situation so familiar and thoroughly understood that there will be a speedy end to the worst aspects of the evil."

According to Adams, Americans were spending some $75 million a year on patent medicines. For their money they got concoctions filled with alcohol, opiates, other narcotics, and "a wide assortment of . . . drugs ranging from powerful and dangerous heart depressants to insidious liver stimulants." Such fraud, he argued, "exploited by the skillfulest of advertising bunco men, is the basis of the trade." He proceeded, at length and in detail, to document the blatant abuse and marketing of a range of dangerous concoctions often brimming with alcohol and suffused with opium or cocaine. The process fed on "faith inspired by [misleading advertisements]," dependent on ignorance and a corrupt, compliant press. Hearst newspapers alone, he reported, received more than a million dollars a year from such advertising. The *Chicago Tribune* received more than $80,000 a year.

Adams's articles, and follow-ups by other publications, were responsible in part for the passage of the Pure Food and Drug Act of 1906. Upton Sinclair's *The Jungle*, a harrowing look at the meatpacking industry in Chicago, published in 1906, likewise galvanized support for federal regulation. The act, signed into law on June 30, 1906, took aim at "the manufacture, sale, or transportation of adulterated or misbranded or poisonous or deleterious foods, drugs, medicines, and liquors." It also paved the way for the creation of the FDA.

"For 15 years or more efforts have been made to throw safeguards around the manufacture and sale of proprietary articles of food and medicine, and it is greatly to the credit of the fifty-ninth Congress and to President Roosevelt that the measure should finally be passed," commented *American Druggist and Pharmaceutical Record* upon passage of the act.

By then the advertising industry was mostly moving beyond patent medicines. It had Bissell carpet sweepers to sell ("Would you pay $2.75 for ten or fifteen years of convenience and comfort?), and luxury cars were the new big thing. In 1907, the Pierce-Arrow was launched with print ads "consisting almost entirely of a lush painting by noted illustrator Edward Penfield," observed Rob Schorman in *Enterprise & Society*. The following year saw ads for the Chalmers automobile headlined "This Astounding Car for $1,500." The Chalmers was "A millionaire's car brought, by mammoth production, down within reach of the many." The advertisements, noted Schorman, were sparse on information but associated the cars with "glamour and success." O'Sullivan's rubber heels did something similar in 1908, claiming that its product bridged "the chasm between the barefooted savage and the civilized man."

The value of mass-marketed propaganda and the impact of emotionally charged appeals were being increasingly appreciated by marketers, and the onset of World War I lifted the industry and its influence to an unprecedented level.

Tim Wu, in *The Attention Merchants: The Epic Scramble to Get Inside Our Heads*, pointed to Great Britain's campaign to recruit soldiers as a particularly skillful use of advertising propaganda. The most memorable ad, also used as a poster, was a direct appeal from Secretary of State for War Lord Kitchener. "Your King & Country Need You: A

Call to Arms" read the headline, followed by text announcing the need for an additional 100,000 men for the regular army. "Lord Kitchener is confident that this appeal will be at once responded to by all those who have the safety of our empire at heart" concluded the message. Another version of the poster featured a stylized picture of Kitchener along with the words YOUR COUNTRY NEEDS YOU, which was a forerunner of the American Uncle Sam poster proclaiming, I WANT YOU FOR THE US ARMY.

The posters were wildly popular. Kitchener achieved his enlistment goal within two weeks, leaving an enduring impression on marketeers everywhere. "There was something about the British and American use of advertising for official purposes that cleansed the practice of its tainted reputation," argued Wu, who noted that Adolf Hitler, who was also paying attention to the successful American and British propaganda effort, admired "its simple presentations of 'negative and positive notions of love and hatred, right and wrong, truth and falsehood' " and, "given his chance . . . thought he could do even better."

The war ended with the advertising industry more powerful than ever. According to the historian Daniel Pope, large magazine advertisers increased spending by some 20 percent from 1916 to 1917, and it continued to grow, even as the industry's take on consumers continued to evolve: "The image of the rational consumer who could be convinced by facts was giving way to the view of the short-sighted, unreasoning buyer to be persuaded by appeals to a grab-bag of instincts or inclinations." There was an increasing focus, in short, on the subconscious, on bypassing the process of rational thought.

As Wu pointed out:

Bringing subconscious anxieties to the fore was the inspired brilliance behind the great campaigns for mouthwash and toothpaste, two products largely unknown before the 1920s.

"Halitosis—makes you unpopular" was the headline of

Listerine's campaign. Originally a disinfectant, invented for medical usage on the battlefield, the brown liquid had also been marketed as a floor cleaner. But in the 1920s, under new management, the manufacturer presented it as a cure for a devastating problem countless Americans were unwittingly afflicted with.

"No matter how charming you may be or how fond of you your friends are, you cannot expect them to put up with halitosis (unpleasant breath) forever. They may be nice to you—but it is an effort."

. . . The campaign was a masterpiece of demand engineering, and between 1922 and 1929, the Listerine company earnings grew from $115,000 to more than $8 million.

That era gave birth to a new generation of reformers, consumer advocates thoroughly convinced that the past reforms were inadequate in the face of the juggernaut that had become the advertising industry. Prominent among them were Stuart Chase and Frederick J. Schlink.

Chase was a certified public accountant, a director of the Labor Bureau and a former Federal Trade Commission investigator. Schlink was a former research engineer and physicist at the United States Bureau of Standards and assistant secretary of the American Standards Association. In 1927, they authored *Your Money's Worth*, one of the more explosive works of the era.

The book began with a series of rhetorical questions: "Why do you buy one make of automobile rather than another? Why do you draw up beside a filling station pump which is painted red rather than one which is painted yellow? Why do you buy the tooth paste you are using . . . ?" Such knowledge about consumer items, they argued, was simply beyond the reach of ordinary consumers: "Even the most expert today can have knowledge of only a negligible section of the field." In the end, they concluded, "We are all Alices in a Wonderland of conflicting claims, bright promises, fancy packages, soaring words, and almost impenetrable ignorance."

The success of the book led Schlink to form Consumers' Research, which launched the *Consumers' Research Bulletin*—which, in 1936, spawned a break-off group called Consumers Union, which ultimately became *Consumer Reports*. The consumer movement ignited by the book endures to this day. The book was one of many forces behind the passage of the 1938 Wheeler-Lea Act, an amendment to the Federal Trade Commission Act that authorized the FTC to restrict unfair or deceptive acts, including false and misleading advertising. But in the end, the book had little impact on the business of marketing dreams.

Some people complained not just about the quality and misleading nature of ads but about their quantity. How, one listener asked, could people enjoy the radio experience if they had to listen to "totally irrelevant advertisement every two minutes?" But for the most part, people were willing to put up with the ads. Nor did ads hinder the acceptance of television.

In 1955, Thomas Coffin, the market research manager of the National Broadcasting Company, noted that two out of three homes were equipped with TVs. "No parallel can be found in any major industry for the rate at which the medium has grown."

Although reliable studies were scarce, some researchers saw evidence that TV owners, compared to nonowners, "knew less about current affairs" and had a "penchant for passive, spectator recreation," wrote Coffin. They were also less likely to read. And not surprisingly, they were more likely to buy products advertised on TV. Coffin wondered whether TV's ability to shape buying behavior could also affect behavior "in such areas as citizenship and community participation." He cited research indicating that it might.

The important lesson of the early television age was that people were not nearly as rational as they thought. "Basically, how a product makes you feel is as important as what it does," acknowledged Dee

Madigan, an Australian advertising executive and author of *The Hard Sell: The Tricks of Political Advertising*. Before advertisers became enlightened, explained Madigan, they assumed "that people spend time reading and thinking about advertisements." But "we discovered that the last thing an advertisement should do was actually encourage rational thought. . . . Encouraging consumers to *think* actually reduced the chance of getting them to buy."

Network psychologists and advertising executives were not alone in recognizing how easily emotions overpowered facts. Vance Packard, a newspaperman and magazine writer turned book author, closely examined practices becoming popular in the advertising industry. The result was *The Hidden Persuaders*, a 1957 bestseller that warned of an advertising industry that was exercising mind control over consumers. "The use of mass psychoanalysis to guide campaigns of persuasion has become the basis of a multimillion-dollar industry. Professional persuaders have seized upon it in their groping for more effective ways to sell us their wares—whether products, ideas, attitudes, candidates, goals, or states of mind," he charged. He wrote at length about a "depth approach to influencing our behavior" and "engineering" compliance. Ruthless politicians, manufacturers, and their enablers were, as he saw it, amorally preying on people's weaknesses: "Certain of the probers . . . are systematically feeling out our hidden weaknesses and frailties in the hope that they can more efficiently influence our behavior." Researchers were learning, he claimed, how to respond to eight "hidden" needs: emotional security; reassurance of worth; ego gratification; creative outlets; a sense of power; love; a sense of roots; and immortality.

The book was generally reviewed favorably, although some critics accused Packard of sensationalizing his research.

In a fifty-year retrospective of *The Hidden Persuaders* published in the *Journal of Advertising*, Professor Michelle R. Nelson concluded that "many of the issues discussed by Packard remain timely 50 years later. Now there is empirical research to substantiate some of the sensational claims." Nelson was especially intrigued by Packard's take on the "threat to democracy" when public officials, inspired by advertising techniques, "appealed to the irrational, emphasized image and personality, and treated public issues like items in a supermarket."

That controversy continues to this day, as does the debate over the impact and efficacy of advertising—political and otherwise—that appeals more to emotions and prejudice than to reason. As politics grows increasingly polarized and fact free, that debate will only get hotter.

It has been raging full tilt since the presidential campaign of 1988, when Republican George H. W. Bush's team seized on the story of a Black convict who had been released on furlough—during which he went AWOL, committed armed robbery, and raped a White woman. Bush's team decided that focusing on the Black rapist was the perfect way to go after Democrat Michael Dukakis. The ad campaign, which prominently featured photographs of the criminal, Willie Horton, was widely viewed as masterfully playing to racism and fears of Black violence without actually referring to race.

Princeton University political scientist Tali Mendelberg observed, "The Horton appeal was . . . about race rather than crime; it mobilized whites' racial prejudice, not their worries about crime. The consequences of this mobilization were greater resistance to government efforts to address racial inequality, heightened perceptions of racial conflict, and greater resistance to policies perceived as illegitimately benefitting African Americans."

Before he died of a brain tumor in 1991, former Republican Party chairman Lee Atwater wrote an article in *Life* magazine apologizing to Michael Dukakis—not for the Willie Horton ads but for insulting remarks Atwater had made that referenced the ads. "Like a good general, I had treated everyone who wasn't with me as against me," he acknowledged.

A perhaps even more baneful influence than the Willie Horton ad was the "swiftboating" campaign waged against Democratic presidential candidate John Kerry in 2004. On behalf of Republican candidate George W. Bush, operatives attacked Kerry, a genuine bemedaled war hero, with claims that he had lied to get his medals and had betrayed his men. The effort—despite being rooted totally in lies and despite Kerry's desperate attempts to get out the truth—was incredibly effective. It demonstrated that even in the face of clear refutation, repeating lies at an ever-increasing volume could wreak grievous harm both on the target and on the truth.

Packard would likely not be surprised by either Willie Horton or swiftboating. They were a natural evolution of the trends he identified. But he would likely be somewhat baffled by the internet, which takes the challenge posed by appeals to emotion rooted in disinformation to totally new levels.

Its very architecture allows people to wallow in whatever propaganda they prefer, even as it insulates them from competing ideas; its algorithms almost always value emotions over intellect; and its exploiters, who have an unprecedented ability to target the most vulnerable, have contributed to the creation of a society in which common and reasoned dialogue is virtually impossible and in which those who are least able to protect themselves are subject to the most cynical manipulation.

In 2017, Facebook made news around the world after the *Australian* newspaper revealed that it was helping advertisers target teenagers based on their emotional state. As the *Sun* of England reported, Facebook "figured out when kids as young as 14 felt worthless or insecure. By tracking posts, it could also identify if they were worried about body image or feeling overwhelmed. The data, shared with advertisers, allowed the social media giant to target them for a 'confidence boost.'"

The revelations provoked an immediate apology from Facebook.

Whether customers are targeted for a boost of confidence, to buy a useless drug, or to accept a candidate on the basis of resentment as opposed to reason, the evidence is clear that we as a society are witnessing manipulation—often performed by simple algorithms—at an unprecedented level.

In a 2017 article in *Critical Studies in Media Communication*, Brian Ott of Missouri State University observed, "As a mode of communication, Twitter is defined by three key features: simplicity, impulsivity, and incivility," making it the perfect medium for people conditioned to prefer communication that has little to do with nuanced or sophisticated thinking. "To be clear, a Tweet may be clever or witty, but it cannot be complex. . . . By demanding simplicity, Twitter undermines our capacity to discuss and, subsequently, to think about issues and events in more complex ways," he argued.

The result, as Ott sees it, is not just degraded dialogue but a weakening of the social fabric. By encouraging such provocative and yet mindless communication, Twitter doesn't just foster "farce and fanaticism," as Ott put it, but takes us in the polar opposite direction of the constructive, self-correcting, increasingly informed discourse that the First Amendment was created to encourage.

In a 1927 opinion concurring with the unanimous Supreme Court decision in *Whitney v. California,* Justice Louis D. Brandeis penned one of the most famous passages in American jurisprudence:

> Those who won our independence believed that the final end of the State was to make men free to develop their faculties, and that, in its government, the deliberative forces should prevail over the arbitrary. . . . They believed that freedom to think as you will and to speak as you think are means indispensable to the discovery and spread of political truth; that, without free speech and assembly, discussion would be futile; that, with them, discussion affords ordinarily adequate protection against the dissemination of noxious doctrine; that the greatest menace to freedom is an inert people; that public discussion is a politi-

cal duty, and that this should be a fundamental principle of the American government.

Brandeis's opinion, ironically, was written in upholding the conviction of Charlotte Whitney, whose only sin had been joining the Communist Labor Party. (The Supreme Court eventually decided that membership in a political party did not constitute a crime.) But the idea behind it, that full and free discussion is essential to the American political process, has never been seriously questioned. Yet, that type of discussion is precisely what Twitter prohibits.

"To me, the Age of Twitter virtually guaranteed the rise of Trump. Public discourse simply cannot descend into the politics of division and degradation on a daily basis without significant consequence," wrote Professor Ott.

Twitter banned Donald Trump permanently in 2021—an act that, in many circles, was met with relief, and even gratitude. But it is not just Trump's noxious rhetoric that made Twitter a threat to democracy. Nor, for that matter, is Twitter the only problem.

Even had Twitter never come into existence, people would be increasingly turning to social media for information about current events. A Pew Research Center study in 2016 found that 62 percent of adults in the US relied on social media for news. In 2021, Pew released a new study showing that 86 percent of adults in the United States "say they get news from a smartphone, computer or tablet 'often' or 'sometimes.'"

The news sources used on digital devices varied widely. "About two-thirds of US adults say they get news at least sometimes from news websites or apps. . . . About half (53%) say they get news from social media, and a much smaller portion say they get news at least sometimes from podcasts (22%)."

Some experts wonder whether the shift toward social media is affecting not only the quality of news consumed but the very ability to consume complex information.

In 2015, a Microsoft study found that the average human attention span had dropped from twelve to eight seconds between 2000 and 2015. "Humans now have a lower attention span than goldfish," reported *The Times* of London, which added, "Researchers found that the top four factors affecting our attention are media consumption, social media usage, technology adoption rate and multiscreen behaviour, such as watching TV while texting."

In *Antisocial: Online Extremists, Techno-Utopians, and the Hijacking of the American Conversation,* journalist Andrew Marantz described his book as a tale of how "entrepreneurs, motivated by naivete and reckless techno-utopianism, built powerful new systems full of unforeseen vulnerabilities, and how a motley cadre of edgelords, motivated by bigotry and bad faith and nihilism, exploited those vulnerabilities to hijack the American conversation."

Whereas traditional news executives attempted to deliver information arguably deemed to be in the public interest—news that, by some ethical criteria, was considered fit to print—the decision-making power, as Marantz saw it, was being given over to an amoral technological Darwinism.

On the web, practically the only thing that mattered was that content provoke emotions—the more intense, the better. Those high-arousal, "activating emotions," drive clicks, likes, and shares. As Marantz put it, "From the standpoint of sheer entrepreneurial competition, what matters is not whether a piece of online content is true or false, responsible or reckless, prosocial or antisocial. All that matters is how many activating emotions it can provoke." And activating emotions are aroused more by fake news than by real news, more by hostility than by cordiality.

Researchers from the Massachusetts Institute of Technology published an explosive study in *Science* in 2018 documenting the truth of

Marantz's assertion. "When we analyzed the diffusion dynamics of true and false rumors, we found that falsehood diffused significantly farther, faster, deeper, and more broadly than the truth in all categories of information," wrote Soroush Vosoughi, Deb Roy, and Sinan Aral. They also discovered that it was not simply algorithms but human choices that accounted for the rapid spread of misinformation: "Contrary to conventional wisdom, robots accelerated the spread of true and false news at the same rate, implying that false news spreads more than the truth because humans, not robots, are more likely to spread it." They added, "The greater likelihood of people to retweet falsity more than the truth is what drives the spread of false news, despite network and individual factors that favor the truth."

The rise of social media—and the rampant misinformation, victim blaming, and anger those media enable and encourage—is occurring at a time when the political advertising and communication industries have become more skilled than ever at promoting lies and selling fantasy as reality.

This is a moment made for someone like Donald Trump, who benefited not only from the rise of social media but from the fascination of the so-called establishment press with public figures who thrive on being outrageous. "Journalists are attracted to the new, the unusual, the sensational—the type of story material that will catch and hold an audience's attention. Trump fit that need as no other candidate in recent memory," noted Professor Thomas E. Patterson in an analysis for Harvard University's Shorenstein Center on Media, Politics, and Public Policy. Although a Donald Trump presidency was not inevitable, the rise of someone like him was. And his success as a political figure, his ability to sell outright lies to his followers—to convince them, most notably, that he won an election he actually lost—ensures that he will not be the last of his breed.

Like it or not, we are stuck in an era when methods once relegated to the marketing of such things as mouthwash are now used to sell presidents, and when the web, once seen as a source of democratization and unbiased information, has become an enabler of bigotry, grievance, and ignorance.

General Leonard Wood was a man ahead of his time. There was nothing illogical about the idea of using techniques honed selling soap to promote a possible president of the United States. That Wood didn't pull it off and Trump did says much about how the United States has changed in a hundred years.

By almost any relevant criteria, Wood was infinitely more qualified than Trump. In his second speech at the Republican Convention, Governor Henry Allen celebrated Wood's credentials:

> You ask for a businessman. We present to you the record of four years as governor of Cuba, a record which gained him international fame as the most successful civil administrator the country has known. Leonard Wood's services in Cuba constitute a page of history which records the cleanest and most unselfish thing one nation ever did for a needy people. . . .
>
> The vague longing for a businessman for president will not be satisfied by one who knows only business. The president must understand world affairs and the crossing and re-crossing currents of social and economic aspirations. . . .
>
> When the great war broke upon the consciousness of the American people with a terrific shock, it found that Leonard Wood had been preparing. . . . This man was no whimperer. Not an hour was lost sulking. No word was wasted in criticism. Not an instant in mourning over personal disappointment.

In many ways, Trump is the opposite of Wood. Trump had no real government or diplomatic experience; he certainly was not known for having a clean, unselfish record; he didn't accomplish much as a businessman other than to inherit a thriving company and survive a series of bankruptcies and unsavory allegations; and he was definitely a braggart and "whimperer" given to sulking and publicly mourning over imagined slights.

Nevertheless, he was thrust upon the world by the marketing geniuses of *The Apprentice*, who substituted fiction for reality, and presented him—and sold him to the public—as the business wunderkind and guru he never was. He, of course, had a little help from the government of Russia and from a former director of the FBI. Also, unlike candidates of the Wood era—thanks to reforms made in the nomination process for presidential candidates after Hubert Humphrey received the Democratic nomination in 1968 without winning a single primary—Trump did not have be vetted by party insiders. Instead, he took his message directly to the people via primaries covered by a press that found him irresistibly entertaining.

As Professor Stephen Knott points out, Trump was not at all what the Founders had in mind for a president. But the Founders also never would have imagined that their carefully cooked up plan for an Electoral College (calculated to produce candidates deemed competent by polite society) would end up giving disproportionate power to an unrepresentative, unaccountable, partisan political minority. And they certainly could not have foreseen how marketing, advertising, and new forms of media would allow a mediocre man to make himself into a titan.

Given the advances in those fields and Americans' susceptibility to emotional appeals laced with racism—it's perhaps not especially remarkable that in Donald Trump, Americans elected a president who saw no value in either truth or complex thought and whose values have less in common with George Washington than with George Wallace, a demagogue who flourished in the days when a bigot (at least in southern states) could pass himself off as a savior.

12

REPEATING THE PAST, CREATING A FUTURE

Americans had never imagined anything quite like the Donald Trump presidency, although in many ways we had been building toward it all along.

A profane man with an incessant need for flattery and coddling, Trump was a familiar face by the time he decided to run for president. His TV show had a lot to do with that. As the host of *The Apprentice*, he had been welcomed into millions of homes weekly. He was cast as a supertalented manager who suffered no fools but whose standards were so high and whose skills so exceptional that even celebrities and Harvard MBAs stood in awe of his competence. They presumably desired nothing more than to remake themselves in his image—or at the very least sit at his knee and absorb his secrets.

Because Trump was already well known, *The Apprentice*, which debuted in January 2004, was highly anticipated—all the more because its creator, Mark Burnett, had been the force behind *Survivor*, a reality show that had become a megahit. His new show would have the bonus of starring one of the most recognizable and controversial businessmen in America. The October before it aired, the *New York Times* described the program as " 'Survivor' Meets Millionaire." And producers made clear that it was to be a mega-advertisement for Donald Trump.

"This is Donald Trump giving back," Burnett told the *Times*, going on to credit Trump with making the United States a richer and better place: "What makes the world a safe place right now? I think it's American dollars, which come from taxes, which come because of Donald Trump."

That was, of course, long before it became known that the Trump legend was largely fiction—that the story about getting a million-dollar loan from his father and converting it into a multibillion-dollar empire was about as accurate as the myth of Midas turning all he touched into gold. As the *New York Times* revealed in its brilliantly reported investigation in 2018, reality is very much "at odds with the story Mr. Trump has sold in his books, his TV shows and his political life." Indeed, far from paying taxes that made America a better place, Trump was being revealed as more of a leech than a patriotic, altruistic benefactor.

The tale about the million-dollar loan is simply a lie. As the *Times* put it, "Mr. Trump received the equivalent today of at least $413 million from his father's real estate empire, starting when he was a toddler and continuing to this day. Much of this money came to Mr. Trump because he helped his parents dodge taxes."

Trump's prominence, in other words, stems from having had a father wealthy enough to keep him afloat as he made a name for himself. In the area of self-promotion, in marketing himself and his name, he did indeed show real talent, which made him a natural for a TV show passing off a pampered—and largely incompetent—heir to a great fortune as a brilliant self-made businessman.

The reviews of his first show were mixed. The *Atlanta Journal-Constitution* complained that it was too much Trump: "The first few minutes of 'The Apprentice' makes one thing crystal clear: You will see, hear, think, dream, imagine and vomit the name Trump." The *Philadelphia Inquirer* opined that for a business-themed reality show, it was weirdly detached from reality: "[No] sane boss in real life would choose an apprentice this way." *The Washington Post* deemed it "Not good but not precisely bad." The *New York Times* was intrigued by the phoniness of it all: "It sometimes seems as though Donald Trump is to business what the Venetian Resort in Las Vegas is to Venice—a fun, cheesy caricature of the real thing."

Despite the lukewarm reviews, the show was a hit. More important, it positioned Trump as the master of all he surveyed, "a demigod," in the words of *Boston Globe* writer Matthew Gilbert. His NBC biography certainly made him sound like one. He was a self-made billionaire genius, a "deal maker without peer," an "ardent philanthropist," and the "very definition of the American success story."

No future politician could have experienced a better launch. Before Trump asked for a single vote from the public, *The Apprentice* had positioned him as a possible savior of America. And that reputation stuck. As an analysis by a research team at the University of Maryland put it, "Ask Americans and many of them will describe [Trump as] a self-made billionaire, a business tycoon of unfathomable success. In research recently published in *Political Behavior*, we found that voters are not simply uninformed about President Trump's biographical background, but misinformed—and that misinformation has serious political consequences."

Trump, of course, loved the narrative. Indeed, he insisted on presenting himself as a self-made financial business genius and guru, and when the time was right, he took advantage of the reputation NBC had carefully constructed, a reputation firmly rooted in exaggeration, distortion, and lies, to reintroduce himself to Americans as the only possible person who could set things straight. "Nobody knows the system better than me [long pause], which is why I alone can fix it," he told adoring fans at the 2016 Republican National Convention.

But before he announced his run, before he got to the convention, he dragged Barack Obama through the mud, trying his best to paint Obama as an illegitimate president, a pretend American who was actually Kenyan and who, despite his ineligibility to become president, had somehow hoodwinked the unsuspecting hordes. Like Trump's reputation as a brilliant businessman, that campaign was based on lies. But that did not matter.

Where he got wind of the rumor about Obama's citizenship is unclear. Trump wasn't the first to make the claim. Reporters who have looked into the matter give that honor to Andy Martin, an obscure political activist who perennially (and unsuccessfully) ran for office.

In *A Culture of Conspiracy: Apocalyptic Visions in Contemporary America*, Michael Barkun named another possible source. In March 2008, a contributor to the conservative website *Free Republic* "who identified himself or herself as FARS, in addition to claiming that Obama had taken his Senate oath on the Koran, also stated 'that Obama's mother gave birth to him overseas and then immediately flew into Hawaii and registered his birth as having taken place in Hawaii.' "

The exact origins of the rumor may be murky, but evidence of Trump's exploitation of it is abundantly clear. As Sidney Plotkin explained in *Veblen's America: The Conspicuous Case of Donald J. Trump*, "The 'sizzle' crackled more for Trump than for [Andy] Martin." Indeed, for Trump, spreading the slur became nothing short of a mission.

In an interview with Fox News' Sean Hannity in April 2011, Trump claimed to have hired investigators who were in Hawaii looking into Obama's citizenship. When pressed on what they had found, he responded, "I don't want to say that now. But it is going to be very interesting. But I don't want to say it now, Sean. . . . I'd much rather be talking about how China is ripping us off."

Later in the interview, he doubled down on his lies: "Six weeks ago, I started really looking into it. He's got a certificate of live birth. That's by the way, despite what certain liberals [say], that's not a birth certificate. It is a big, big step lower." He continued with the nonsense: "Look, he's got a grandmother in Kenya who said he was born in Kenya at the hospital. Then there was bedlam in the room, bedlam. I don't mean like a little, you know, because he was close to becoming president. And there were a lot of people in that room, and he was being, she was talking to a reporter with a lot of handlers."

All of it was fabricated, but Hannity let Trump rattle on. And his claims had an effect. In early 2011, just over half of Republican primary voters believed that Obama had been born outside the United States. "Any thought that the birther theory has been put to rest can be thrown out the window with this poll," observed Dean Debnam, the president and CEO of Public Policy Polling, which had conducted the poll.

The plethora of lies emanating from Trump and others about Obama's birthplace became such a distraction that in late April 2011, the White House released copies of his birth certificate (the long form as well as the short form), proving he had been born in Honolulu, Hawaii.

That day, Trump was visiting New Hampshire, America's first political primary state. After his helicopter landed in Portsmouth, he held a press conference and pretended that his pack of lies constituted a form of public service: "Today, I am very proud of myself, because I have accomplished something that nobody else has been able to accomplish. I was just informed while on the helicopter that our president has finally released a birth certificate. I want to look at it, but I hope it's true—so that we can get on to much more important matters, so the press can stop asking me questions. He should have done it a long time ago." That from a man who had never released his own birth certificate and, for that matter, dared not release his school or college transcripts, although he insisted (to immense skepticism) that he had been a top student.

Frank DiPrima, a lawyer writing for the Daily Kos website, claimed to have been told repeatedly by William T. Kelley, a deceased marketing professor at the Wharton School of the University of Pennsylvania, that "Donald Trump was the dumbest goddam student I ever had." Since Kelley is dead, it is impossible to verify what he said, but numerous journalistic attempts to verify Trump's academic record have yielded no evidence that he was a good student.

In April 2011, the *Mail on Sunday* noted the release of Obama's birth certificate and observed, "It is a belated and perhaps somewhat anxious attempt to head off a claim that has dogged his presidency even before his formal swearing-in." The *Mail* theorized that the release was "aimed at what promises to be the most damaging intervention yet for his hopes of re-election next year: a book by Jerome Corsi called *Where's The Birth Certificate?*, which it is claimed will expose glaring holes in Obama's account of his past."

The article noted that Trump, who "has positioned himself to run for the White House next year with a campaign fueled almost entirely by questions about Obama's place of birth," had a huge stake in the story.

Corsi had been one of the key figures behind the swiftboat smear, which, by all evidence, was one reason John Kerry had lost the 2004 election. But the book had no discernible impact on the Obama campaign.

Trump decided to sit out the 2012 campaign, likely because he had realized he couldn't beat Obama. But he also had the last laugh. In August 2016, The Hill website reported that a majority of registered Republican voters "still doubt President Obama's citizenship."

Even though the birther hoax was revealed as an outright lie, Trump learned, as the swiftboat connivers had and as marketers have known all along, that lies, even transparent lies, work. They can also get you a hell of a lot of attention.

———

After sitting out the 2012 presidential contest, Trump was raring to go in 2016. In January 2015 in Trump Tower in New York City, he officially announced his candidacy and previewed the type of campaign he would run. In that appearance, he lashed out at Latin Americans: "When Mexico sends its people, they're not sending their best. . . . They're sending people that have lots of problems. . . . They're bringing drugs. They're bringing crime. They're rapists. And some, I assume, are good people. . . . It's coming from more than Mexico. It's coming from all over South and Latin America, and it's coming probably—probably—from the Middle East."

He made clear from the first moment of his campaign that he was running not so much against Hillary Clinton as against Mexicans and others crossing the southern US border and against Muslims from the Middle East.

Indeed, it's striking how similar Trump's rhetoric during his campaign announcement—and also his subsequent complaints about immigrants from "shithole countries" such as Haiti, El Salvador, and Africa as opposed to Norway—was to the testimony of the eugenicist Madison Grant, who had told Congress roughly a century earlier that there was "no good reason why the Latin-American countries to the south of us, which in some cases furnish very undesirable immigrants, should have preferential treatment over, let us say, Scandinavia or England," and complained that Mexican immigrants were of low intelligence and "overwhelmingly of Indian blood."

Given his focus, it stood to reason that one of Trump's first acts as president was to try to ban immigration from several countries with large Muslim populations.

More than any other presidential candidate in modern times, Trump made clear that he was the candidate of White anger and minority exclusion, the White nationalist who would keep America safe for real Americans, White Americans. No longer need they tremble in fear of the dark hordes huddled at the border, plotting in Arab countries, or running rampant in the United States' urban centers. John Wilkes Booth, who faulted Abraham Lincoln for not acknowledging, "This country was formed for the white man," presumably would have been quite comfortable with Trump and his complaints about "shithole countries" and his yearning for Norwegian immigrants.

Why, in 2016, did Americans look for salvation in the buffoonish figure of an unqualified candidate who had nothing but contempt for many people of color—beginning with President Obama? Much of the answer lies in his tenure on *The Apprentice*. He was packaged as a selfless, supremely confident managerial genius. His image essentially immunized him against his own behavior, even if that behavior seemed irrational or wildly inappropriate. Many people simply weren't prepared to believe that he was as clueless as he often sounded. Also, he happened to come along at a time when many White Americans were growing nervous—and he spoke directly to their concerns.

From the beginning of his candidacy, Trump appealed to "white racial fear and resentment," noted the political scientist Alan I. Abramowitz in *The Great Alignment: Race, Party Tranformation, and the Rise of Donald Trump.*

> His description of Mexican-American immigrants as criminals and rapists, his repeated promise to build a wall along the Mexican border and make Mexico pay for it, his proposal to deport 11 million undocumented immigrants, his false allegation that thousands of Muslims in New Jersey had celebrated when the twin towers of the World Trade Center came down on September 11, 2001, and his call for a ban on foreign Muslims entering the country were in many ways the centerpiece of his campaign.

Abramowitz's research told him that the growth in White resentment had not materialized out of nowhere; much of it had been triggered by the Obama presidency, which had provided an eager audience for a racialized message that was "far more explicit than those used by earlier GOP candidates like Ronald Reagan and George H. W. Bush."

It had also, no doubt, been aggravated by demographers' projections that minorities are on the verge of taking over the country—or at least of becoming a majority of the population. As a 2018 report from the Brookings Institution put it, "The new statistics project that the nation will become 'minority white' in 2045." That supposition is nothing short of frightening to a considerable number of Americans who equate minorities with crime, violence, poverty, depravity, and doom.

Trump's style, his blatant appeals to racial animosity, are not typical of a US president. But it is nothing new in US politicians. Think of Orval Faubus mobilizing the Arkansas National Guard to block nine Black schoolchildren from entering Little Rock's Central High. Think of George Wallace, surrounded by eight hundred Alabama state troopers, standing in front of Foster Auditorium at the University of Alabama to block two Black students from enrolling. Think of Lester Maddox, the owner of the Pickrick fried chicken restaurant in Atlanta, pulling a gun on and labeling as "Communists" two Black students who requested service at his restaurant—a gesture that won him the KKK's endorsement and propelled him into the governor's mansion.

Think back even further, to 1860, when the social order seemed threatened to another generation of Whites. In a speech in Lexington, Kentucky (as reported by the *Louisville Daily Journal*), John C. Breckinridge, the fourteenth vice president of the United States, the Southern Democratic presidential candidate, became the official voice of southern resentment: "The Governor of Ohio refuses to restore a man indicted for felony, because, he says, it is no crime under the laws of Ohio to steal a negro. . . . Where in the north can the Fugitive Slave law be executed? . . . Look at the encroachments, year after year. Look at how you are environed and closed in upon, State after State . . . the Constitution thrown with contempt into our faces: the purpose avowed to exclude the South from all the vast common domain of the Union."

Now think of Donald Trump, ordering peaceful protesters to be violently cleared from Washington's Lafayette Square so he could march in peace to St. John's Church to pose with a Bible or threatening to send federal troops to put down antiracism protests in "Democrat cities" because "We can't let this happen."

How did such a cavalcade of race-baiting, angry politicians win acclamation and wide acceptance? It's the same reason that Ku Klux Klan leader David Duke almost became governor of Louisiana, his ascent stopped only by the refusal of Black voters to accept him. Appealing to emotion works, and few emotions are as potent, or as likely to shut down the mind, as anger fueled by racial resentment.

Go back to Theodore Bilbo, segregationist, senator, and two-term governor of Mississippi and the author of *Take Your Choice: Separation or Mongrelization*. Bilbo was hailed by the pastor at his funeral in 1947 as "one of America's greatest men and surely Mississippi's greatest." *The Washington Post* obituary writer had a different take, noting that Bilbo's peddling of "fear and distrust of minority groups" could have won an even larger following had he been more polished and better packaged.

Trump was, in a sense, the fulfillment of that apprehension, a more capable peddler of fear and distrust, buoyed by the best marketing effort network television, social media, and modern advertising could muster.

Whether any of these demagogues believe what he says is almost beside the point. As the *Post* observed of Bilbo, his rhetoric "was dictated by what he felt was necessary to preserve and strengthen his reputation as the one unyielding defender of white Protestant Americanism." There is an element of that in all demagogues; the theater is at least as important as the substance.

As governor, Maddox, who campaigned on racism, presided over an administration the *New York Times* called "perhaps the most liberal in Georgia's history." When I met George Wallace, confined to a wheelchair, years after his glory days, he confided (with who knows what degree of self-reflection, honesty, or sincerity) that his best friend was his Black caretaker.

The issue has little to do with whether, in their hearts, Trump and the other demagogues peddling racial division believe what they say. They know that such tactics work, that gullible followers will reward their displays of racial grievance, even as everyone doggedly denies racism's very existence. They want to ensure that Whites are not trampled on or even inconvenienced as society rushes forward to accommodate Blacks. It is precisely the same concern Andrew Johnson expressed in 1866—a time when southern Blacks had no rights that Whites were obliged to respect—as he vetoed the civil rights bill which, as he saw it, would "establish for the security of the colored race safeguards which go indefinitely beyond any that the General Government has ever provided for the white race."

That gains for racial minorities can only come at the expense of Whites is a viewpoint as old as the nation itself. And the blame perhaps lies with our Founding Fathers, who saddled Americans with an impossible task: embracing the notion that all men are created equal but also that some are significantly more equal than others. When Thomas Jefferson proclaimed "all men are created equal," he never expected to be taken literally. He apparently meant for the statement to be followed with an unseen comma and an unnoticed phrase, something along the lines of "except for certain people, who obviously and definitely are not equal." Some scholars believe that Jefferson never meant the phrase to apply to individuals at all but that it was about a collective equality, in the sense that American colonists were entitled to the same right of self-government as sovereign nations, argued the Stanford University historian Jack Rakove.

The historian Pauline Maier pointed out that one reason Congress initially rejected a bill of rights—what James Madison called a "prefix"—was because of a "perception by certain slave states that assertions of universal human equality and rights were a recipe for trouble."

In *Notes on the State of Virginia*, Jefferson raised and attempted to answer the question of whether Blacks and Whites could live together outside the framework of slavery. In the end, he suggested that Blacks should be deported and Whites brought in to do the work heretofore done by the enslaved. As discussed previously, he saw profound and inherent differences between the races, beginning with the color of Blacks, which "is less beautiful than that of whites" and including their inferior ability to reason. You cannot read that and believe for a second that the man who wrote "all men are created equal" actually believed those words or even accepted the fact that Negroes were really men.

In the notorious Dred Scott decision, as we have seen, Justice Roger Taney made clear that the Declaration of Independence's promise of equality had nothing to do with "the enslaved African race" since "the conduct of the distinguished men who framed the Declaration of Independence would have been utterly and flagrantly inconsistent with the principles they asserted" had Blacks been comparable, in any way, to themselves.

Whatever Jefferson actually meant when, after editing George Mason's draft, he ended up with "all men are created equal," he created a terrible dilemma for the acolytes and others who came after him. They could either decide that Thomas Jefferson was consciously lying or that he expected everyone to understand that Blacks were not quite human. And if Blacks and other non-Whites were not really men, if they instead existed somewhere on a continuum between men and untamed beasts, there was absolutely nothing wrong with taming them, enslaving them, beating or killing them, with imposing the myriad of cruelties that slavery demanded.

After the South lost the Civil War, Americans preferred to rehabilitate the Whites who had betrayed the Union rather than elevate Blacks and create the race-blind nation they knew the Founders had never intended to exist. And when the KKK sprang into existence and took on the role of White supremacy's enforcers, many Americans believed that it was performing a useful service.

It says something about the complexity of that extraordinary moment that even the most die-hard Confederates never insisted that the South had actually won the war or that Lincoln had never really been elected and was therefore not the true president. They were not so deluded as to launch a "stop the steal" movement to award the presidency to John Breckenridge. They just thought that they, by force if necessary, could bring more Americans around to their way of thinking, which is not to say they did not have their own delusions—or perhaps just rationalizations.

In an article published in 1871, the *Baltimore Sun* explained, from the viewpoint of Whites in Spartanburg, South Carolina, why the KKK was needed. In a phrase, it was because Blacks had totally ruined Reconstruction: "Robberies by negroes were of almost daily occurrence, barn burnings were frequent, and for these atrocities nobody was punished. . . . Do you feel any surprise at the whites becoming bitter and revengeful?"

Whites were supposedly subject to arbitrary arrest in such high numbers that "in some cases the cotton was on the field unpicked when every male on the farm, from fifteen years upwards, was arrested," putting their crops at risk. Also, with no men to defend them, "hundreds of white women and children [were] completely at the mercy of the negroes." It's no wonder that such "an oppressed and plundered people" came up with the KKK for the unimpeachably honorable purpose of restoring stability.

A writer in the *Louisville Courier* made a similar case, arguing that the Klansmen, comprising "a majority of the best men in the communities where they were established," existed only to "resist oppression" and oppose "depredations."

A former North Carolina Klan member told the Select Committee of the Senate to Investigate Alleged Outrages in the Southern States that he and his friends had joined the Klan "to protect ourselves and our property and our wives." The committee also heard testimony from a witness who alluded to "Ku-Kluxing negroes," meaning Blacks who dressed up in Klan regalia to commit crimes for which Whites would be blamed. The Klansmen, in short, were not at fault; they were simply defending themselves from unendurable horrors.

A minority report from the Senate committee insisted that race relations in the South had been great before northern carpetbaggers had "infested" the region and endeavored "to destroy the sympathy and good feeling which had always existed between the white people and the black people of the South . . . when the blacks worked cheerfully and faithfully to support the wives and children of the confederate soldiers."

The reborn Klan of the 1920s made essentially the same claim: that it was a good organization that believed in God and country and was all for racial harmony.

In 1922, after being granted, then denied, a permit to march in the "colored section" of Hyattsville, Maryland, the Klan responded by dropping copies of a publication from an airplane explaining the purpose of the KKK. The document, according to the *Afro-American*, dealt "with the color question entirely, every article referring to social equality, intermarriage, etc. On the first page is the cartoon of a colored boy and a white girl going to school hand in hand with a shadow of Abraham Lincoln over them. Under the cartoon is printed, 'Freedom. Yes. But Not This.'"

A reader of the *Herald of Gospel Liberty*, a Christian newspaper based in Massachusetts, became enraged in 1923 by the newspaper's criticism of the Klan. She wrote a letter in response: "If you have not read up [on] this subject, you had better before you condemn it; for at least one-half of our ministers belong to this great organization. It was founded by a minister of the gospel, and is based upon the twelfth chapter of Romans. I want you to know it is not against the Catholic Church, the Jew, or Negro; but is purely American. . . . It is filling the churches here and stands for law and order—not mob violence."

The idea that things had been just fine in the South before north-ern carpetbaggers had come and put crazy ideas into the heads of Blacks was not only used to defend the KKK but adopted years later by White opponents of integration who blamed "outside agitators" in-stead of their own racist policies for racial conflict. Characteristic was the portrayal of Klan members as salt-of-the-earth patriotic Americans whose only sin was being too eager to defend God, country, and White womanhood. Members of White Citizens' Councils presented them-selves as an even more refined class, eminent leaders of their respective communities whose reputations were above reproach. "The Councils have an almost self-conscious desire for respectability," wrote David Halberstam in *Commentary* in 1956. In reality, "[Their] only serious purpose is to fight the National Association for the Advancement of Colored People."

They were also not above concocting phony incendiary scandals in their quest to demonize Blacks and crush Black aspirations. As the his-torian Neil McMillen related, one former Arkansas state senator and White Citizens' Council member used a fraudulent tape recording as a recruiting device. The recording, supposedly of an address given to an NAACP audience in Mississippi, "left little to the imagination about the 'real' motives behind the Negro's quest for social equality." The tape had been put forth as proof that "the NAACP and their insolent agitators are little concerned with an education for the 'ignorant nig-ger'; but, rather, are 'demanding' integration in the white bedroom." Eventually the tape was exposed as a fake.

The idea that it is possible to brutalize people of color, to deny them access to the ballot, to refuse to accept them in communities, and still be a morally upright person is pervasive. It has become normalized in American thought, as has the idea that inequality in society is not any-one's fault; it's just the way things are—precisely the same arguments that made heroes of the KKK, lent credibility to eugenicists and politi-cians who declared war on Chinese immigrants, Japanese Americans, and assorted other minorities whose fundamental crime was hoping to be treated with decency.

In a sense, it all goes back to Jefferson, who was incapable of envisioning America as a multiracial democracy. The fact that he could not do so does not diminish his stature as a great man; it just makes him a flawed great man.

But Americans like to see things in black and white. We tend to see people as either good or bad. Gray areas are difficult for us. So it is easier to ignore or rewrite history than to accept it as it is, in all its nuanced complexity. The problem is that, in doing so, we leave ourselves with no acceptable explanation for our current divisions other than to blame those who dare to point them out—and who use history to explain them.

———

The tragedy of COVID-19 forced the subject of racial inequality back into the news, as one study after another showed that Blacks, Latinos, and indigenous populations were much harder hit than Whites.

Ahmad Khanijahani, a certified health data analyst at Duquesne University, found that Blacks and Hispanics were roughly three times as likely to get the disease and also three times as likely to die from it as Whites were. He also noted that Blacks and Latinos were more likely to live in poor, segregated communities and work at jobs they could not do remotely and that Blacks were disproportionately employed as "essential" workers and therefore less likely to be able to avoid coming into contact with infected people.

The problems of concentrated poverty, divergent health profiles, and unequal access to medical care long predated the political rise of Donald Trump. Even a competent president, fully committed to human equality, would have had a difficult time handling the unexpected crisis.

Initially, certain areas were much harder hit than others. The disease seemed to affect mostly states and cities Trump loathed, the

"Democrat" cities he wanted to flood with federal troops, the very cities about which he tweeted, "Leave Democrat cities. Let them rot."

Did Trump's hatred of such places account, at least in part, for his lackadaisical (and then absurdly hyperpartisan) response to COVID-19? Is that why hundreds of thousands died from a disease that a responsible leader would have met with action, clarity, and honesty?

I doubt it. I suspect that at base, the problem was just too complicated for a man with Trump's limited abilities who lacked empathy and compassion and easily got sucked into the messy morass of his own ego-gratifying disinformation. He simply was not up to the job. That job required a person who respected science and was capable of mobilizing the nation around a grander purpose than slamming political enemies.

But Trump was not elected for his competence. He was elected, at least in part, because he excelled in getting people to despise one another. And that fact raises the question of how we can cope as a country when one of our two major political parties is more interested in telling lies, spreading propaganda, encouraging culture wars, and fomenting racial conflict than in anything remotely resembling responsible governance.

The appearance of the various variants of the coronavirus and the lives that they needlessly claimed made clear, particularly in states whose leadership treated the disease as just one more excuse for partisan brinkmanship, that our penchant for such polarizing behavior is killing us.

———

Stuart Stevens, a Republican operative and the author of *It Was All a Lie: How the Republican Party Became Donald Trump*, began his book with a confession: "I was drawn to a party that espoused a core set of values: character counts, personal responsibility, strong on Russia, the national debt actually mattered, immigration. . . . What a fool I was. All of these immutable truths turned out to be mere marketing slogans."

Instead, he discovered that his party was little more than a "white grievance party" and realized that the most relevant lesson was one he had learned early on, that "race was the key in which much of American politics and certainly all of southern politics was played."

There was a time when Republicans were not seen as race-baiting opportunists. In the 1850s, as discussed previously, they were considered so sympathetic to the antislavery cause that they were derisively called "Black Republicans." Even after Franklin D. Roosevelt inspired the great Black migration to the Democratic Party, Republicans continued to garner a decent amount of Black support.

That changed in the early 1960s with the rise of Barry Goldwater. In a speech to the Republican Strategy Conference in November 1961, Senator Goldwater addressed the question of the Negro vote. Republicans, he said, could not "outpromise the Democrats. Consequently, we're not going to get the Negro vote as a bloc in 1964 or 1968." He recommended that the party give up its courtship of Negro voters and "go hunting where the ducks are." He also spoke against federal enforcement of school integration and promised to "bend every muscle to see that the South has a voice on everything that affects the life of the South."

Bruce Galphin, a columnist for the *Atlanta Constitution*, opined, "Sen. Barry Goldwater's statement that he would support an amendment placing control over school integration in the hands of the states just about read Negroes—Northern and Southern—out of the party." The *Pittsburgh Courier* concurred: "Senator Barry Goldwater virtually filed papers for divorce of the Republican party from the Negro during the GOP 'strategy conference' drawing delegates from 12 states here last week."

In the end, Goldwater lost the 1964 presidential race to Lyndon Johnson. He won only six states: his home state of Arizona plus Louisiana, Mississippi, Alabama, Georgia, and South Carolina. His southern victories were nonetheless significant, as they broke the trend of the South voting for Democrats.

Nixon realized that the way to cement the southern vote was to dive deep into the quicksand of racial polarization. Ever since then (despite push back from moderate Republicans), the party has been doubling down on that bet—to the extent that current party rhetoric evokes a surreal sense of déjà vu, taking one back 150 years or more.

Trump and his followers would have been right at home in the KKK of the 1870s or 1920s or in the White Citizens' Councils of the 1950s; for their message is essentially unchanged. It is still largely about fear of marauding minorities out to destroy White culture, of radicals intent on disrupting the comfortable status quo.

The former president has been credited with having the instincts of a political savant for realizing that such a strategy would work in 2020. But it hardly takes a genius to realize that blatant appeals to prejudice work. They have done so since long before the Civil War. They worked after World War I. They worked after World War II. They worked during the civil rights movement. So of course they work now—as long as one does not go too far, as long as one is not too blatant, as long as one gives oneself room to claim that the message comes from a person pure of heart.

But why are we stuck in this de facto racial war that has never made any sense—at least not for most people?

Certainly, for owners of big plantations or of enterprises hungry for cheap labor, slaveholding was a logical way to go. But those people were never anywhere near the majority of Americans or even the majority of White people. Nonetheless, vast numbers of working-class Whites relinquished all reason in order to side with wealthy, race-baiting opportunists who never had their interests at heart. In doing so, they embraced the idea that skin color was the preeminent marker of identity and value. Many continue to worship at the feet of those who tell them that their very survival is somehow contingent on keeping America White.

Although that premise was never plausible, it impelled confused people to bomb little girls in a church and to murder a Black boy wrongly accused of flirting with a White woman.

Today, of course, Americans are not so crude. Self-declared protectors of civilization no longer routinely lynch Black men for pursuing White women—in part because (certain) White women made it clear that they wanted to be pursued. But voting is another thing: a massive movement has arisen in the Republican universe to do everything short of repealing the Fifteenth Amendment in order to deny Black and Brown citizens that constitutional right. And the reason is the same as it has always been: that "they" will destroy America's greatness.

That premise has proven to be a powerful driving force for violence. Indeed, the chaos that broke out in Charlottesville in 2017 and ended in anti-racism protester Heather Heyer's death—and with Trump's declaring that there were good people and bad people on both sides of the issue—began with a young White man who had apparently been traumatized by learning that Whites would eventually become a minority.

Jason Kessler, a thirty-three-year-old man who lived with his parents and had once supported Barack Obama, suddenly became a White supremacist. He organized the rally in Charlottesville to protest the removal of a statue of Confederate leader Robert E. Lee, but also, said Kessler, as a way of "standing up for our history" and, presumably, for a whiter-than-anticipated future.

The idea that the United States will become irremediably transformed because Blacks, Asians, and Hispanics collectively reach a certain population level is more than a bit odd. For starters, given the constitutional design of the Senate, House of Representatives, and Electoral College and the way representation is apportioned in the United States, a numerical majority does not necessarily add up to the power to control the country. George W. Bush and Donald Trump both can attest to having won the presidency even after losing the popular vote. Also, the Senate, because it apportions representation by state, as opposed to by population, is a fundamentally undemocratic institution and one that will continue to be skewed toward smaller states dominated by Whites—barring the ratification of a constitutional amendment to change things.

Moreover, definitions of race are constantly evolving. A race that is non-White today might well be White tomorrow. Over the years, Jews, Italians, Arabs, and others who were considered non-White, or not quite White, have been magically welcomed into whiteness. That phenomenon is not going to change, whatever the presumptively dominant racial group is by the time 2045 rolls around.

Moreover, the idea that society will somehow self-destruct when Whites are no longer in charge assumes that Whites invariably know what they are doing or at least will govern wisely. I see no evidence that either of those propositions is true.

———

In his first inaugural address, on January 14, 1963, George Wallace declared:

> Today I have stood, where once Jefferson Davis stood, and took an oath to my people. It is very appropriate then that from this Cradle of the Confederacy, this very Heart of the Great Anglo-Saxon Southland, that today we sound the drum for freedom as have our generations of forebears before us done, time and again down through history. . . . In the name of the greatest people that have ever trod this earth I draw the line in the dust and toss the gauntlet before the feet of tyranny and I say, segregation now, segregation tomorrow, segregation forever.

At the time, according to the National Education Association, Alabama ranked 47th (among the states) in per capita personal income, 46th in percent of high school graduates, and 41st in percent of "substandard high school teachers." It would have made a hell of a lot more sense for Wallace to have promised a good education to all Alabamians or a program to ensure that decent people got decent jobs. Instead, he was cheered for giving the KKK and its angry progeny permission to wreak havoc upon Blacks.

Trump was elected for much the same reason and was granted a much larger stage. And what did he do with all his power? Instead of attacking an epidemic that was killing his countrymen in droves, he blathered nonsense about consuming household cleaners to cure the disease and warred on those wearing protective masks. He demonized Brown people at the border, condemned "shithole" countries, and railed against those protesting police mistreatment of minorities, while salivating over a fantasy of massive immigration from Norway. He also prattled nonsense about getting Mexico to pay for a border wall to keep out immigrants and about the dangers of Antifa, even as he invited Russia to sabotage the US elections.

Trump never delivered on his promise to make America great again or even explained when it had been great. Was it when Emmett Till was murdered in Mississippi? Or perhaps when John Lewis was beaten on the Edmund Pettus Bridge? Or maybe it was at the Battle of Bull Run. Maybe we witnessed his vision of greatness in January 2021, when a mob inspired by his lies invaded the Capitol, causing several deaths and scores of injuries, even though Trump later insisted, "It was zero threat, right from the start. . . . Some of them went in, and they are hugging and kissing the police and the guards."

When seen from Trump's perspective, the entire world looks different than when it is viewed through a normal person's eyes—which makes one wonder what all the people prepared to fight on his behalf actually think they are fighting for and raises the infinitely more difficult question of why such a man, with such fuzzy yet divisive goals, engenders support from such a large proportion of at least a segment of the public.

Trump's ratings, which had always been low with Democrats, dropped even lower after the January insurrection, but he continued to poll well among Republicans. A poll by the Pew Research Center taken just before Joe Biden's inauguration had 57 percent of Republican and Republican-leaning respondents agreeing that Trump should remain "a major political figure." Sixty-four percent believed that he had likely won the election he had clearly just lost.

What that says, of course, is what we already know: that Trump's lies work, at least on a great many people. But it also implies something considerably more worrisome, which is that the culture of lying, misrepresentation, and misdirection is likely to be his legacy to US politics. The party he reshaped in his image is not going to change easily.

What may be even more troubling is that Trump and his allies have established, beyond a doubt, that political lies can be extremely lucrative. An organization headed by a lawyer who became prominent pushing the idea that Trump really won the election pulled in a fortune. As a *Washington Post* headline summed it up, "Sidney Powell group raised more than $14 million spreading election falsehoods." Indeed, Trump himself has made millions from such lies. As *Forbes* magazine reported in January 2021, "Former President Trump pulled in $255.4 million in political donations from his supporters in the eight weeks following the 2020 election . . . but much of this money—which was solicited to fund challenges to the outcome based on specious claims of voter fraud— will likely be put to other uses."

For reasons both financial and political (ethics and morality apparently have nothing to do with such calculations), Trump's acolytes seem committed to continuing down the road of lies and racial resentment.

They responded to an electoral defeat by targeting Black and Brown voters for exclusion; and, some 150 years past the Reconstruction Era, they decided to rerun the playbook put together by the side that lost the Civil War.

That resulted in a wave of new legislation in so-called red states calculated to disenfranchise people of color, taking aim at absentee voting, restricting the use of drop boxes, adding new ID requirements, and even denying water to voters patiently waiting in line. All of those measures were supposedly aimed at combating election fraud that only ever existed in the minds of Trump and his acolytes. In March 2021, *The Washington Post* counted 250 new proposed laws offered by Republicans in forty-three states that, as the *Post* put it, could amount "to the most sweeping contraction of ballot access in the United States since the end of Reconstruction."

All of this effort is aimed at helping a minority party maintain its power any way it can; but it is also aimed at the very idea of democracy. And its success depends on figuratively refighting the Civil War.

Campaigns based on racism are inherently rooted in dishonesty because they invite us to attribute traits to our fellow citizens that they don't possess. They invite us to see Mexicans as rapists and Blacks as a menace to society. They prepare us to see victory in the exclusion of our fellow Americans. So we ignore real issues as we obsess over dark villains who exist only in our minds.

This is not just partisanship, it's mindless tribalism; it's "us against them" run amok. It's madness that has persisted for more than 150 years. At some point this sickness must end.

I believe that it will end. The question is when.

———

I am writing these words in November 2021. Much of the current news has been of two criminal trials that some believed would tell us much about the state of race and justice in America.

One was the trial of Kyle Rittenhouse. He was seventeen in August of 2020 when he left his home in Antioch, Illinois, to go to Kenosha, Wisconsin. His mission was to protect property from people protesting the police shooting that left Jacob Blake, a twenty-nine-year-old Black man, partly paralyzed. Rittenhouse had reached out to a friend who had acquired a semi-automatic rifle for the teen, who was too young to legally possess such a weapon. Rittenhouse took the rifle and joined a group of vigilantes pledged to defending public property near the Kenosha County Courthouse. Before the night was over, Rittenhouse had killed two unarmed men and wounded another, who himself was carrying a handgun, in what Rittenhouse subsequently claimed was self-defense. All his victims were White.

Police at the scene didn't consider Rittenhouse a threat. Indeed, they initially seemed to blame protestors for the deaths. "Persons who were out after curfew became engaged in some type of disturbance, and persons were shot," declared Kenosha police chief Daniel Miskinis. After shooting the men, Rittenhouse left the scene with his weapon and returned to Antioch, where he was arrested the next day.

The second trial was of three White men accused of killing a Black jogger, Ahmaud Arbery, in February 2020. Gregory and Travis McMichael, father and son, were residents of Satilla Shores, a small, overwhelmingly White neighborhood in Glynn County, Georgia. They spotted Arbery, whose presence apparently so unrattled them that Travis got his Remington shotgun and his father grabbed a .357 Magnum revolver. They jumped into their truck and took off in pursuit. A neighbor, William "Roddie" Bryan, Jr., got into his own truck and helped to corner Arbery, an unarmed twenty-five-year-old. The confrontation turned violent and ended with Travis McMichael shooting Arbery.

A Glynn County police officer responded to a report of "shots fired and a male on the ground bleeding out." Gregory McMichael was himself a former Glynn County police officer, which may have accounted for the unusually considerate treatment the three men received. Instead of arresting the men, the cops let them go home.

The local district attorney recused herself because she knew Gregory McMichael. A second district attorney recused himself after asserting that if Travis McMichael had been attacked, he had the right "to use deadly force to protect himself." Only after the video of the conformation taken by Bryan went viral, did a third prosecutor bring the matter before a grand jury, which indicted the three men for murder.

Both trials took place in November 2021 and were extensively covered by the press. The juries contained one Black person apiece. Other Blacks in the jury pool had been removed, for supposedly non-racial reasons, following challenges by defense attorneys.

In the months following his arrest, Rittenhouse was lionized by the right-wing media and by various political figures. On November 19, 2021, he was fully exonerated. Following the acquittal, Donald Trump, Jr., posted a doctored photo of Rittenhouse receiving the Medal of Honor from former president Trump. Rittenhouse's lawyer told CNN that, although Rittenhouse believed himself to be legally innocent, he regretted the incident: "Kyle said, if I had to do it all over again and had any idea something like this could happen, I wouldn't do it."

Less than a week after Rittenhouse walked free, a jury found all three defendants in the Arbery case guilty of murder.

As is the norm in such highly publicized trials, news organizations and media personalities searched for larger lessons. Various observers found hope in the Arbery verdict. The case showed that violence was unacceptable and "hopefully quells white supremacist ideology," commented one legal expert to *Vox* news. On the other hand, the Rittenhouse verdict caused concern. "His acquittal has reinvigorated support on the right for armed responses to racial justice protests and unrest," declared the *New York Times*.

Reporters and commentators are essentially required after a big legal case to find significance in the outcome, whether or not there is, in reality, any deep meaning to be found. I doubt there is any deep meaning here.

Sure, the fact that three White men were convicted of killing a Black man means that we are no longer in the time of Emmett Till— when Whites, particularly in the South, could kill Blacks with absolute impunity. But then, Emmett Till's killers in 1955 had no video to deal with, and no real evidence against them, since the police had not bothered to conserve any. So, it was easy for the all-White jury, after sixty-seven minutes of deliberation, to declare Till's killers innocent. As the *Baltimore Sun* noted, the jury apparently accepted the defense theory "that rabblerousers put a Negro body—dead some days—in the river and falsely ballyhooed it as Till's."

The jury foreman, a farmer named J. A. Shaw, explained why the accused were found innocent. "We had a picture of the body with us in the jury room and it seemed to us the body was so badly decomposed it could not be identified," he told the press. Asked about the testimony of Till's mother, who identified the body as that of her son, Shaw dismissively replied, "If she had tried a little harder she might have got out a tear."

Thank God, we are no longer in that era. But had there been no video, it's more than likely that the killers of Ahmaud Arbery also would have been exonerated. Local prosecutors certainly were in no rush to prosecute them. So even though we are no longer in 1955, it's not clear how much we should be celebrating where we are.

Both the Rittenhouse and Arbery cases raise troubling questions. Why do a considerable number of White males apparently think it is okay for them to grab guns and go into full vigilante mode when Black men do nothing more provocative than appear in neighborhoods where they are deemed not to belong? Why is it so easy for juries and the public at large to see innocence in the eyes of White armed provocateurs? Why was it considered brilliant lawyering for the prosecutor, in the Arbery case, to minimize any mention of racism, lest she alienate right-wing jury members? Why, after these senseless killings, do we end up repeatedly having the same discussion about how far our country has come in matters of race? And why do so many of us think it is perfectly okay for armed men to insert themselves into situations where they have no legitimate role, and where they can serve no productive purpose? And why, for God's sake, would any sane person celebrate and attempt to make a role model out of a misguided, ill-disposed, armed young man who apparently needs counseling much more than a medal from Congress?

We, as a people, as a country, are much better at agonizing briefly over these tragedies than at taking measures to ensure they don't occur. In the same way we offer thoughts and prayers to children killed in school shootings, we offer empty platitudes to people of color killed simply because they were not White in a place where whiteness is the norm.

We have a pattern of agonizing (briefly) whenever atrocities or riots take place. We call together so-called experts, and earnestly seek their opinions. Then the crisis passes, and we move on, and we forget whatever it was they had to say—until the next time tragedy strikes.

Rather than figuring out what is wrong with our approach, some Americans argue for simply shutting down racial discussions altogether—at least those that don't celebrate the compassion and generosity of Whites of all eras. They ask that a book written by a Black Nobel Prize winner be banned simply because it shows how awful slavery was. They demand the removal of teachers who dare to teach American history, in its true complexity, because they somehow equate teaching truth with trying to make Whites hate themselves.

When the very social critics who refuse to talk honestly about race celebrate racialized violence against nonviolent protestors or encourage violence toward non-White politicians, when ignorance about unpleasant aspects of history is deemed a virtue, when otherwise intelligent people doggedly refuse to acknowledge how out past affects our present, it's difficult to see how we, as a society, derive any meaningful lessons from the tragedies we so regularly, albeit briefly, mourn.

———

In 1965, just two weeks after the Bloody Sunday bloodbath in Selma, Alabama, the Rev. Martin Luther King, Jr., led a five-day protest march from Selma to Montgomery, the Alabama state capital. As the *New*

York Times reported the event. "The Rev. Dr. Martin Luther King Jr. led 25,000 Negroes and whites to the shadow of the State Capitol here today and challenged Alabama to put an end to racial discrimination."

Although Governor George Wallace had agreed to meet with a delegation from the group, he refused to allow them on Capitol grounds. Nonetheless, reported the *Times*, King's speech was audible in Wallace's office; and "the Governor was seen several times parting the venetian blinds of a window overlooking the rally."

Standing before the huge crowd, King gave a pep talk for the ages:

> I know you are asking today, "How long will it take?" I come to say to you this afternoon however difficult the moment, however frustrating the hour, it will not be long, because truth pressed to earth will rise again.
>
> How long? Not long, because no lie can live forever.
>
> How long? Not long, because you still reap what you sow.
>
> How long? Not long. Because the arc of the moral universe is long, but it bends toward justice.

That final phrase originated with Theodore Parker, an abolitionist minister from the 1800s, whose version was "I do not pretend to understand the moral universe. . . . I cannot calculate the curve and complete the figure by the experience of sight; I can divine it by conscience. And from what I see I am sure it bends towards justice."

The sentiment is wonderfully hopeful, and precisely how most of us hope that the universe works. But, in truth, I'm not sure how the arc of the moral universe bends. It seems to bend every which way, often rewarding those who seem least to deserve it. The arc of US demographics, on the other hand, is pretty clear: groups that were once considered minorities are, in fact, gaining a larger and larger share. That is not going to stop in the foreseeable future. And it will, in fact, mean change—not in the way some fear but in the sense that we are ultimately going to have to acknowledge that the United States is not just a White nation. And we are going to have to stop making such a big deal out of something that shouldn't matter.

So-called people of color see race somewhat differently from the way Whites do. It's not that we are smarter, but that we are smart enough to know that *we* are not the problem. We know, from having lived the consequences, that bigotry is not a good thing. And instead of running from acknowledging it, we have no choice but to face it.

Indeed, Americans of all colors have increasingly come to recognize that racial discrimination makes no sense. And it seems that each generation is more enlightened—at least on that matter—than the one that came before. Even many of the elders among us seem to be learning what toddlers seem to sense intuitively: that the differences of race are trivial and nothing worth fighting about.

There is a multiracial array of people who want to be free of the preconceptions of the past, who recognize that acknowledging the impact of racism—past and present—is not the source of our division but perhaps of our deliverance, and who accept that a society that refuses to acknowledge its missteps is likely to keep going down the same dark path.

One day we will be free enough of this racial sickness, distant enough from the evils spawned by enslavement, to collectively and creatively focus on what really divides us—on why so many people support an economic-political order that grants nearly 40 percent of the country's wealth to 1 percent of the population, that pays the CEOs of so-called Fortune 500 companies more than three hundred times what their workers receive, that provides a few moguls with enough money to buy private shuttles in which they joyride into space and others with barely enough to pay their bus fare to work, that promotes survival-of-the-fittest health care policies that leave many ordinary Americans unable to pay for their kids' education or their own medical care, that impoverishes young people for trying to get through college.

Since the dawn of time, powerful people have excelled at deflecting blame and responsibility away from themselves and toward those who are least capable of defending themselves. Perhaps when we stop focusing on supposed ethnic differences, we can focus on what we can do about that.

Thomas Jefferson had a country to build and realized that it would be built largely on the backs of enslaved people. So he justified treating people as animals while simultaneously articulating a philosophy of equality, liberty, and freedom. But things have changed. Today, there is no human bondage to justify.

The reason for the Founders' rationalizations no longer exists— other than to cater to the insecurities of those who are determined to blame their problems on people who had nothing to do with those problems. Intelligent people are coming to see that catering to that un-reasoning resentment is killing us—which is why I believe that we can see, beyond the horizon, a day when this particular source of division will no longer exist.

What is more worrisome is another divide that has become impossible to ignore: that is the divide between those who accept facts and those who do not, between those who respect science and those who prefer not to, between those who try to weigh long-term consequences and those who don't.

As has become unavoidably clear, the outcome of some of the major issues before us has a lot to do with the quality of our thinking, with our ability to put preconceptions aside and digest reality. The Founders didn't much believe that ordinary people were good at doing so, which is why they built so many safeguards into this republic, why they separated the masses from the real levers of political power, why we don't elect presidents directly, and why it took a constitutional amendment to get direct election of senators.

As the political scientist Demetrios Caraley put it, "the Founders saw democracy as equivalent to tyranny of the majority or even mob rule." They preferred "what they called a 'republic,' because in a republic . . . the government is delegated 'to a small number of citizens.' This small number would be able 'to refine and enlarge the public views' and their wisdom could 'best discern the true interest of their country.' "

Over the centuries, the United States has moved closer to the ideal of a true democracy, where, at least in theory, every voice has a right to be heard. At the same time, issues have become more complicated and more difficult to follow, and disinformation has become epidemic. We have reached a dangerous point where much of the public can't be bothered with the task of getting to the truth and therefore puts its trust in political propaganda and conspiracy theories, while dismissing even self-evident facts. This road leads to nowhere good. Perhaps, as many fear, it will lead to the end of the democracy we thought we were building.

What is the antidote to the threat of willful ignorance, to the apparent inability of so many to think clearly or to distinguish blatant lies from reality? The challenge to our educational system is clear: it must become better—fast—at teaching critical thinking.

Unfortunately, certain politicians are applying maximum pressure to ensure that critical thinking is the last thing institutions of learning encourage. With laws aimed at prohibiting the teaching of uncomfortable ideas, they are determined to keep students as complacent as possible—even if that complacency is rooted in close-minded thinking and ignorance. Ignorance may not be bliss, such politicians seem to assume, but it is infinitely better than having young people question the ways of their elders.

The challenge to the larger society perhaps is to understand that the most serious danger to democracy lies not in our differences but in our failure to see beyond them.

A large group of Americans has bought into a very specific and odd idea of democracy, complete with a new Bill of Rights that includes the right to forgo wearing face masks during an epidemic, which implies the right to spread infectious diseases; the right to buy and bear powerful military-grade arms, which implies the right to recklessly endanger the lives of ordinary citizens and schoolchildren; the right to reject duly elected leaders in deference to defeated candidates, which implies the right to ignore the will of the majority; the right to dismiss the evidence of global warming and science in general, which implies the right to kill the planet and pollute the environment; the right to lie about whomever and whatever they like without regard to any harms that doing so might cause; and the list goes on.

The beauty of this new Bill of Rights is that it requires no process of ratification; it just requires a willingness to jettison the idea that rights come with responsibilities and that democracy belongs to more than the anointed few.

How should a democratic-leaning society respond to this? There are certain obvious options. One is to submit to the tyranny of the minority and accept the consequences; another is to attempt to compromise, profess faith in bipartisanship, and hope that the politics of ignorance is a passing fancy; another is to refuse to concede an inch to a belligerent minority that believes its self-selected rights are the only rights that matter

We have faced similar choices before. Thanks to the experience of the Framers in drafting a constitution and to the experience of Republicans of another age in reconsidering Reconstruction, we have a pretty good sense of what it means to bend to those with no respect for the rights of others. We know that to compromise with those who are intent on perpetrating immorality is to make the ultimate deal with Satan. We have learned that meekly giving way to bullies is nothing more or less than appeasement.

Our long and still ongoing fight for recognition of our common humanity regardless of gender, skin color, or ethnicity has also taught us that the capacity to fight vile ideas and bad behavior is infinite, even in the face of crushing odds, especially if we keep faith with the proposition, yet unproven, that the arc of democracy eventually bends toward the common good.

ACKNOWLEDGMENTS

Although I only recently realized it, I have been thinking about this book since I was a teenager. It was then that I discovered, and was deeply influenced by, the writings of Lerone Bennett, Jr., a historian and executive at *Ebony* magazine.

When I was barely out of high school, Bennett published a series in *Ebony* titled "The Making of Black America" in which he proposed an idea that has haunted me to this day. "A nation is a *choice:* it chooses itself at fateful forks in the road," he wrote.

Over the years, Bennett became a mentor and a friend. Although we occasionally disagreed, I always respected his intellect and integrity, and I often found myself reflecting on his assertion. Recently, I have wrestled with the question of why my fellow citizens, after electing Barack Obama, chose to install Donald Trump as his successor.

That question became a motivating obsession behind this book. For that, I owe Lerone Bennett. I also owe Gwendolyn Brooks, a magnificently generous Pulitzer Prize–winning poet who was the first person of stature to tell me (indeed, to insist) that I was fated to become a writer—and who, in so doing, changed the course of my life.

Many people played roles in the production of this book, or in helping to refine the ideas that inform it, beginning with Tracy Sherrod, my editor. In an age when publishers tend to require meticulously detailed blueprints for a book, complete with conclusions that have not yet been reached, with the hope of minimizing risk and surprises, Tracy continues to trust her instincts and the competence of her writers to take a good idea and mold it into something worth reading. Without her, this book would not exist. Nor would it exist without the faith and support of Lee, my wife, and Elisa, my daughter, whose boundless confidence in me has sustained me when my own has occasionally wavered.

My dear friend Martin Garbus realized early on that I would occasionally need a quiet place to work without any possibility of disturbance. So, he gave me his temporarily unoccupied apartment to use as my own whenever the need arose; and he inspired me with a daunting challenge. "I am determined to see at least one important book come out of this apartment," he said.

Over the years, I have accumulated a posse of creative thinkers who helped me through this process. Thank you, Elyse and Steve Montiel, Sonia Sotomayor, Anthony Romero, Elijah Anderson, Nadine Strossen, Calvin Sims, Henry McGee, Bobby Austin, Carlos Cortes, Jeanne Sahadi, Everette Dennis, Rick Smith, Charles Whitaker, Tim McChristian, Carroll Bogert, Ieva Massengill, Sue Gronewold, Kirkland Vaughans, Beate Arnestad, Diane McWhorter, and Walter Watson.

Thanks also to my agent Don Fehr, whose wise guidance has been essential through this and my last two books.

Also, I thank my colleagues Kate Black and Eric Cox, who not only have served as ideal sounding boards but who, in throwing in with me on my Renewing American Democracy project, freed me up enough to do what I had to do to get this book done.

I owe a huge debt to Geoffrey Cowan, director of the Center on

Communication Leadership and Policy at the University of Southern California, and to Kimberly Cline, president of Long Island University. In addition to being an endless source of creative ideas, Geoff provided essential institutional support for both this book and also for Renewing American Democracy. His own writings led me to ponder the role of state primaries in presidential elections. Kim not only cheered on my literary efforts, she eagerly took on the task of institutional responsibility for the set of ideas that became Renewing American Democracy. She and her associates—Tweed Roosevelt, Christopher Fevola, and Andy Person, in particular—have been a godsend.

Finally, I thank Alexa Allen, editorial assistant at Amistad, whose cheerful competence has made her a joy to work with.

As is customarily and correctly the case, I claim any errors or mistakes in this book as my own.

SELECTED BIBLIOGRAPHY

A NOTE ON SOURCES

In writing this book, I drew on hundreds of sources—including newspaper, magazine, and journal articles; books; court decisions; and congressional documents. I have listed below some books that I found particularly helpful. I did not do the same with newspaper or other periodical sources because I did not want to burden the reader with numerous superfluous pages of text.

I came of age in a time when authors of serious books spent endless hours consulting the *Readers Guide to Periodical Literature* prior to heading into the stacks or spending long days hunched over microfilm or microfiche. I still do that, or something equivalent to it, when I visit the Library of Congress or specialized libraries in search of certain materials that are not digitized or widely available. For the most part, however, newspaper and journal research has become a digital enterprise.

A good researcher, equipped with the proper databases, can easily find the source material for quotes or a random bit of information from a newspaper or a journal without need of a formal citation. For that reason, I have opted not to include those here.

Books are a little different, although they are becoming increasingly available and searchable on digital databases as well. Nonetheless, the reason for consulting a book is generally more complicated than simply trying to run down an intriguing quote. Books can lead one on unforeseen and interesting journeys. So, I believe there is some small service in listing those books that I have found valuable in producing this volume. I hope that, by doing so, I will encourage you to explore some of the texts below.

Alan I. Abramowitz, *The Great Alignment: Race, Party Transformation, and the Rise of Donald Trump* (New Haven: Yale University Press, 2018).

James C. Ballagh, *A History of Slavery in Virginia* (Baltimore: The Johns Hopkins Press, 1902).

Lucy G. Barber, *Marching on Washington* (Oakland: University of California Press, 2002).

Michael Barkun, *A Culture of Conspiracy: Apocalyptic Visions in Contemporary America* (Oakland: University of California Press, 2013).

Michael Les Benedict, "Andrew Johnson," in Ken Gormley, ed., *The Presidents and the Constitution* (New York: NYU Press, 2016).

Volker Berghahn, "American and British Businessmen and Attempts to Reconstruct War-Torn Europe, 1918–1922," in Andrew Smith, Kevin Tennent, Simon Mollan, eds., *The Impact of the First World War on International Business* (New York: Routledge, 2017).

A Bill Concerning the Qualifications of Voters or Electors, Hearings before a Subcommittee of the Committee on the Judiciary, US Senate (Washington: Government Printing Office, 1942).

Douglas Blackmon, *Slavery by Another Name: The Re-Enslavement of Black Americans from the Civil War to World War II* (New York: Doubleday, 2008).

William Harris Bragg, "Reconstruction Chapter," in John C. Inscoe, ed., *The Civil War in Georgia: A New Georgia Encyclopedia Companion* (Athens: University of Georgia Press, 2001).

Stuart Chase and F. J. Schlink, *Your Money's Worth* (New York: The Macmillan Company, 1927).

Steven Conn, *History's Shadow: Native Americans and Historical Consciousness in the Nineteenth Century* (Chicago: University of Chicago Press, 2004).

Geoffrey Cowan, *Let the People Rule: Theodore Roosevelt and the Birth of the Presidential Primary* (New York: W. W. Norton & Company, 2016).

Ellis Cose, *Democracy If We Can Keep It: The ACLU's 100-Year Fight for Rights in America* (New York: The New Press, 2020).

Ellis Cose, *A Nation of Strangers: Prejudice, Politics and the Populating of America* (New York: William Morrow and Company, 1992).

Commission on Wartime Relocation and Internment of Civilians, *Personal Justice Denied* (Seattle: University of Washington Press, 1997).

Angie Debo, *And Still the Waters Run: The Betrayal of the Five Civilized Tribes* (Princeton: Princeton University Press, 1940).

Kees van Dijk, *Cleanliness and Culture* (Leiden: Koninklyk Instituut Voor Taal Land, 2012D).

H. Dilbeck, *Frederick Douglass: America's Prophet* (Chapel Hill: University of North Carolina Press, 2018).

Eleanore Douglas, "Herbert Hoover and the Adjustment to the Depression," in *Strategic Retrenchment and Renewal in the American Experience* (Carlisle, Pa.: Strategic Studies Institute, U.S. Army War College, 2014).

Henry M. Flint, *Life of Stephen A. Douglas* (Philadelphia: John E. Potter, 1863).

Lawrence Friedman, *American Law in the Twentieth Century* (New Haven: Yale University Press, 2004).

Alejandro de la Fuente and Ariela J. Gross, *Becoming Free, Becoming Black: Race, Freedom, and Law in Cuba, Virginia, and Louisiana* (Cambridge: Cambridge University Press, 2020).

Alan Gallay, *The Indian Slave Trade: The Rise of the English Empire in the American South, 1670–1717* (New Haven: Yale University Press, 2002.)

Matthew Goodman, *The Sun and the Moon: The Remarkable True Account of Hoaxers, Showmen, Dueling Journalists, and Lunar Man-Bats in Nineteenth-Century New York* (New York: Basic Books, 2008).

Madison Grant, *The Passing of the Great Race* (New York: C. Scribner's Sons, 1916).

René Hayden et al., eds., *Freedom: A Documentary History of Emancipation, 1861–1867* (Chapel Hill: University of North Carolina Press, 2008).

F. Michael Higginbotham, *Ghosts of Jim Crow* (New York: NYU Press, 2013).

Michael Hiltzik, *The New Deal: A Modern History* (New York: Free Press, 2011).

James D. Horan, *The Pinkertons* (New York: Crown Publishers, 1967).

Investigation of Un-American Propaganda Activities in the United States, Hearings before a Special Committee on Un-American Activities, House of Representatives (Washington: Government Printing Office, 1942).

Thomas Jefferson, *Notes on the State of Virginia* (Boston: Lilly and Wait, 1832).

Don Jordan and Michael Walsh, *White Cargo: The Forgotten History of Britain's White Slaves in America* (New York: NYU Press, 2017).

Tracy E. K'Meyer, *Civil Rights in the Gateway to the South* (Lexington: University Press of Kentucky, 2009).

Bandy Lee et al., *The Dangerous Case of Donald Trump* (New York: St. Martin's Press, 2019).

David Levering Lewis, *King: A Biography* (Champaign: University of Illinois Press, 2012).

John Lewis, *Walking with the Wind: A Memoir of the Movement* (New York: Simon & Schuster, 2015).

Dee Madigan, "Advertising and Change: Message, mind, medium, and mores," in Gabriele Bammer, ed., *Change!* (Canberra, Australia: ANU Press, 2015).

Peter C. Mancall and James Horn, eds., *Virginia 1619: Slavery and Freedom in the Making of English America* (Chapel Hill: University of North Carolina Press, 2019).

Jesse McCarthy, *Who Will Pay Reparations on My Soul* (New York: Liveright, 2021).

Charles McGovern, *Sold American* (Chapel Hill: University of North Carolina Press, 2006).

James M. McPherson, *Battle Cry of Freedom: The Civil War Era* (Oxford: Oxford University Press, 2003).

James M. McPherson, *Crossroads of Freedom: Antietam* (New York: Oxford University Press, 2002).

Cameron McWhirter, *Red Summer: The Summer of 1919 and the Awakening of Black America* (New York: St. Martins Press, 2011).

Kenneth Morgan, *Slavery and Servitude in North America, 1607–1800* (Edinburg: Edinburg University Press, 2000).

Philip D. Morgan, "Virginia Slavery in Atlantic Context, 1550 to 1650," in Paul Musselwhite, Peter C. Mancall, James Horn, eds., *Virginia 1619: Slavery and Freedom in the Making of English America* (Chapel Hill: University of North Carolina Press, 2019).

Roy Morris Jr., *Fraud of the Century: Rutherford B. Hayes, Samuel Tilden, and the Stolen Election of 1876* (New York: Simon & Schuster, 2007).

Barton Myers, "Sherman's Field Order No. 15," in John C. Inscoe, ed.,

The Civil War in Georgia: A New Georgia Encyclopedia Companion (Athens: University of Georgia Press, 2011).

John Olszowka, Marnie M. Sullivan, Brian R. Sheridan, and Dennis Hickey, *America in the Thirties* (Syracuse: Syracuse University Press, 2014).

Elaine Frantz Parsons, *Ku-Klux: The Birth of the Klan during Reconstruction* (Chapel Hill: University of North Carolina Press, 2015).

Vance Packard, *The Hidden Persuaders* (New York: David McKay Company, 1957).

Sidney Plotkin, *Veblen's America: The Conspicuous Case of Donald J. Trump* (London: Anthem Press, 2018).

Pearl T. Ponce, *To Govern the Devil in Hell: The Political Crisis in Territorial Kansas* (DeKalb: Northern Illinois University Press, 2014).

Andrés Reséndez, *The Other Slavery: The Uncovered Story of Indian Enslavement in America* (Boston: Houghton Mifflin Harcourt, 2016).

Restriction of Immigration: Hearings Before the Committee on Immigration and Naturalization, House of Representatives (Washington, D.C.: Government Printing Office, 1924).

Angela Saini, *Superior: The Return of Race Science* (Boston: Beacon Press, 2019).

Eric Schickler, *Racial Realignment: The Transformation of American Liberalism, 1932–1965* (Princeton: Princeton University Press, 2016).

Harvard Sitkoff, *Toward Freedom Land: The Long Struggle for Racial Equality in America* (Lexington: University Press of Kentucky, 2010).

Lothrop Stoddard, *The Rising Tide of Color: Against White World-Supremacy* (New York: Charles Scribner's Son, 1920).

Stuart Stevens, *It Was All a Lie: How the Republican Party Became Donald Trump* (New York: Alfred A. Knopf, 2020).

Kristopher A. Teters, *Practical Liberators: Union Officers in the Western Theater during the Civil War* (Chapel Hill: University of North Carolina Press, 2018).

Adam Tooze, *The Great War, America and the Remaking of the Global Order, 1916–1931* (New York: Penguin Books, 2014).

Peter Vasterman, ed., *From Media Hype to Twitter Storm: News Explosions and Their Impact on Issues, Crises and Public Opinion* (Amsterdam, Netherlands: Amsterdam University Press, 2018).

Nancy J. Weiss, *Farewell to the Party of Lincoln* (Princeton: Princeton University Press, 1983).

Ida B. Wells-Barnett, *The Arkansas Race Riot* (Chicago: Aquila, 1920).

David Williams, *The Georgia Gold Rush: Twenty-Niners, Cherokees, and Gold Fever* (Columbia: University of South Carolina Press, 1993).

Bob Woodward, *Rage* (New York: Simon & Schuster, 2020).

Tim Wu, *The Attention Merchants: The Epic Scramble to Get Inside Our Heads* (New York: Vintage, 2016).

INDEX